Cecil Beaton
Stage and Film Designs

Charles Spencer

Cecil Beaton Stage and Film Designs

ACADEMY EDITIONS · LONDON/ST. MARTIN'S PRESS · NEW YORK

DEDICATION

To the memory of my mother who remains as vivid an influence in my life as Esther Beaton has been to her famous son.

ACKNOWLEDGEMENTS

The idea for this book followed an invitation from Sheridan Morley to contribute an essay on Beaton's stage work for *Theatre 73*. I am grateful to him for sowing the seed. Without the enthusiasm and generosity of Sir Cecil Beaton this study would not have been possible. He has not only put at my disposal all his publications, his library of designs and photographs, files, press-cuttings, scrap-books and volumes of sketches but also has given freely of his own time. I thank him for permission to quote from these interviews and from his various writings, and to reproduce both original drawings and many of his superb photographs. Sir Cecil's secretary, Eileen Hose, also has assisted me in every possible way, and I am deeply indebted to her knowledge, efficiency and friendly co-operation. Other photographs in this book were taken by Graham Bush. I also wish to thank *Vogue* for permission to quote or reproduce from their issues. I thank Christine Bernard for reading the manuscript, and, as with all my previous literary efforts, my secretary Hilda Meyer for her patience and skill.

C.S.

First published in Great Britain in 1975 by
Academy Editions 7 Holland Street London W8

SBN cloth 85670 154 8

Copyright © Charles Spencer 1975. All rights reserved

Library of Congress Catalog Card Number 75-24746

Printed and bound in Great Britain at
Balding & Mansell, Wisbech

First published in the U.S.A. in 1975 by
St. Martin's Press Inc.
175 Fifth Avenue New York N.Y. 10010

(frontispiece) Audrey Hepburn in the film of *My Fair Lady*, 1963 (Photo: Cecil Beaton)

Contents

The stage struck child

If Cecil Beaton was not born stage-struck, he certainly achieved the condition very soon after. With his power of almost total recall he can pinpoint the moment of departure. One morning, when barely three years old, he climbed into his mother's bed and noticed a picture-postcard of the actress Lily Elsie on the bedside table. Passion for the theatre and photography, as he puts it, 'were thus engendered at the same moment'. From then on he anxiously awaited the illustrated weekly magazines delivered to the house, in the hope that an image of his favourite would appear. And if not Miss Elsie, he begged in his nightly prayers, then Miss Gertie Millar, or Miss Florence Smithson, two other reigning theatrical beauties; and if not them then the glamorous French star Gaby Deslys.

Nostalgia plays a dominant role in Beaton's artistic consciousness, in all his fields of endeavour, as photographer, diarist and designer for stage and cinema. The theatre, however, above all other artistic experiences, has been the most potent. His earliest and most enduring ambitions were inspired by the theatre, firstly as an actor (an amateur at Harrow and Cambridge, and, for one brief moment of glory, a professional in America); as a writer (the author of one play and a prolific journalist); and as the designer of numerous plays, operas, ballets and films. Even his famous career as a photographer can be said to have been inspired by the stage.

Cecil Beaton was born in London on 14 January 1904, the eldest of four children. His two younger sisters, Baba and Nancy, were to become famous as his earliest photographic models. The Beatons had long been timber merchants, and his father, Ernest, inherited part of the family business. His parents occasionally visited the theatre, but his father took it a little more seriously. In his youth he had been an enthusiastic amateur actor, appearing once in a play with the distinguished actress Lilian Braithwaite; in the family circle he was admired for his impersonations of such current matinee idols as Sir Henry Irving, Martin Harvey and Charles Hawtrey. Beaton senior had an album of newspaper cuttings on his theatrical adventures; he regularly took a stage weekly and kept a file of play programmes. On business trips to the United States he would bring back illustrated souvenirs of Broadway productions. All this, his son admits, "gave him an aura of romance for me and whetted my initial appetite for the theatre". His mother's influence came from her taste and sense of design, which Beaton has consulted all his life.

Cecil was four years when he was first taken to the theatre, a matinee performance of *The Merry Widow* at Daly's Theatre. To his dismay the legendary Lily Elsie was indisposed, and he had to make do with her understudy Daisy Elliston. (He forgave Miss Elsie when he met her in later years, lovingly recording her maturer image in portraits and photographs). From then on he became an avid theatre-goer. When not actually in an auditorium, he would study the photographs displayed outside. By chance the family nanny, Alice Collard, was a gifted amateur photographer, exercising her skill on her young brood. Cecil was struck by the 'theatricality' of these snapshots and was determined to try his own hand. One Christmas Nanny Collard presented him with a Box Brownie Camera.

Thus his passion for the theatre was matched by a parallel involvement with photography. After studying publicity shots outside the theatres, or in the fashionable journals, he would pose his

7

Cecil Beaton aged 3 years

Mrs. Ernest Beaton with her four children

Master Beaton with his mother and younger brother

Lily Elsie in *The Merry Widow*, portrayed by the mature Cecil Beaton

mother, sisters, schoolfriends, and even himself, in imitation of well-known stage performers. Students of his photographic career will be aware that these pre-occupations have remained a constant element of his style, from the 'surrealistic' posing of the poet Edith Sitwell, which made him famous at the age of twenty four, to the images of hundreds of actors, society beauties, fashion models and international personalities produced in a long career.

His photography progressed so well that for his twelfth birthday he received a No. 3a Folding Pocket Kodak. By this time he had picked up a few

tricks of the theatrical photographic trade. In particular he studied the work of a contemporary photographer, Miss Compton Collier, who special-ised in shots of leading actresses in their drawing-rooms or gardens. Preparing elaborate picnics, he would entice his family and friends into the garden and with various theatrical props pose them in imitation of Miss Collier's studies of Pavlova, Gladys Cooper or Laurette Taylor.

His first essay in stage production occurred in his tenth year, whilst staying with some aunts in remote Worcestershire. In a box-room he con-structed a toy-theatre from a hat-box and mounted a production of the musical comedy *Oh, Oh, Delphine*. He recalls the preparations in vivid detail:

First I cut photographs of the chorus ladies out of *The Play Pictorial*, painting their faces in full stage make-up. Then the evening dresses were washed with pastel colours and dotted in gold and silver liquid paint that had such a strong acid smell it remains in my nostrils to this day. I faithfully reproduced the rose and wistaria scenery, then turned on an electric torch on the tableau. Characters were pushed on stage by means of tin clips attached to long handles. It remained only to make them perform, which I did by acting all the parts and singing the score myself. Here in remote Arley, my theatrical dreams flourished...

When he was five or six years old a new acquain-tance of the family, a minor professional actress, was invited to dine. Too excited to sleep, Cecil crept out of bed and peered through bannister rails to witness her arrival. Later he was allowed the special treat of meeting the lady in the drawing room. To this day, more than 65 years later, he recalls the dress she wore, made of voile, with white and red-pink stripes. Thirty years after the event, while designing *Lady Windermere's Fan* and searching for a striking visual effect, he thought of that little actress and re-created her peppermint-stick dress.

This delight in decorative detail, preserved by a prodigious memory, marks the whole of his stage career. Like his father, he began to collect pro-grammes and stage magazines, as well as theatrical

The artist as a schoolboy

Drawing by Master Beaton, then
aged 10 or 11 years

Nancy Beaton, aged 13 years,
dressed, posed and photo-
graphed by her elder brother

An early effort at photography, Beaton's sisters, Nancy and Baba, with a friend, c. 1918

photographs. In the theatre his concern was not for plot or dialogue, but for details of scenery, costume and make-up. What fascinated him was the mixture of reality and fantasy, real human beings and real furniture against painted back-cloths. In *The Country Girl* his attention was riveted by real stooks of corn attached to a back-drop on which similar sheaves had been painted, or by an orchard with three-dimensional, artificial apples hanging from a painted tree. On other occasions he studied genuine wistaria trailing on a painted border or artificial roses nailed to sten-cilled ones.

During a holiday in Norfolk the family was taken to see a pierrot troupe at Sheringham. Through the incandescent gas lighting the youthful Cecil memorized the stylised make-up, red dots in the corners of the eyes, blobs of black on the eyelashes. Later in London he would borrow his father's field glasses to study make-up at closer range. This mixture of childish enchantment and the beginning of professional research is illustrated by another holiday memory of the south-coast town of Folkestone. With wide eyes he watched a travel-ling theatrical company arrive at the local theatre, disgorging scenery from huge vans. 'I stood bathed in enchantment as the tall pieces of *The King of Cadonia's* palace were lifted through hangar-like doors.... Next Monday *The Arcadians* would arrive with miraculous woodland sets.'

In many of his later theatrical works, which include ballets based on sea-side events, Edwardian family dramas, and musical plays of life before the First World War, Beaton constantly re-discovered childhood experiences, encrusting visual memories with glamorous colour and decorative detail in an unconscious effort to relive some thrilling moment

of impressionable adolescence.

As a schoolboy, during the First World War, his theatrical visits continued in the holidays. He recalls the famous revue *The Bing Boys*, in which Violet Lorraine and George Robey sang *If You Were the Only Girl in the World* (a duet which Beaton and his school-chum Cyril Connolly repeated in the tea-room of London's Ritz Hotel for the television programme *Beaton by Bailey*, in 1971). What Beaton most recalls from *The Bing Boys* was a contribution by Arthur Weigall, a setting of bright emerald-green chestnut trees, with white terraces, as the background for scarlet costumes. Beaton has always responded to daring colour combinations, hence his admiration for Bakst and Bérard.

It was the theatre which provided the youthful Cecil Beaton with his visual education. By the end of his schooldays at Harrow he had heard of the Renaissance and loved Botticelli; he also knew of the Pre-Raphaelites and found Beardsley thrilling. Beyond that modern art was equated with the Ballets Russes. At Harrow he indulged in photo-graphy and amateur theatricals, making his first efforts as writer, producer and actor in 1921, when, aged 17, he was co-director of *Five Short Plays*, performed in aid of the Harrow Mission. The programme lists C. W. H. Beaton as the adaptor of two stories by O. Henry, in one of which he played the part of Delia. Other roles for Master Beaton were Mrs. Page in Sir James Barrie's *Rosalind* and Mrs. Cubb in *Shepherd's Pie* by Sewell Collins. The programme was completed with a one-act play by Stephen Leacock.

He left Harrow as a 'prize art student' with a flair for caricature and a growing fascination for stage design, but Beaton himself had little confi-

The Beaton family at the seaside, c. 1922-3

dence in these talents. 'Secretly I was as anxious about my future as my father must have been'.

For an understanding of Beaton's career as a stage designer, these early details are of crucial importance. In reconstructing the Edwardian period, culminating in the world-famous *My Fair Lady*, he has often referred to the importance of memory in his creative processes. 'Whenever I am embarking on the designs for a new production, early impressions of the theatre come back to mind, and many of my most successful effects have been dividends that have been paid to me from the past. Some of the most successful dresses have been inspired by memories of early playgoing days'. In theatrical designing there are the poets, who depend largely on their imaginations, pedants,

who recreate the past with encyclopaedic care, and romantics, who establish a mixture of fantasy and fact. Beaton combines elements of all three; he certainly uses imagination and takes considerable care to study the historical period, as his numerous note-books confirm. But far more important to him personally and most effective in his theatrical work is the constant need to recreate the atmosphere of his childhood.

This preference for Edwardiana, more instinctive than calculated and so obsessive that at times Beaton has revolted against it, may be a psychological pull back to the security of childhood, the shared pleasure of parental interests. In his stage work, it certainly represents the most successful expression of his decorative gifts.

Apprenticeship

Beaton usually dismisses his university career as a waste of time. He was down to read History and Architecture but hardly attended a lecture, and in the last two years did virtually no academic work at all. Nevertheless, it was an important period of trial and experiment, stretching his talents and powers, gaining experience and encouragement.

As a stage-designer he is completely self-taught. (In his fifties Beaton attended the Slade School, London, to study oil painting, his only formal academic training in the arts.)

At Cambridge he acted in and designed four plays, playing 'female' leads in all-male casts, and took part in undergraduate revues. The reception of his work was almost universally positive, and within a short time he was a member of the committee of the Marlowe Society. His 'aesthetic' appearance, with long hair, scarlet ties and gauntlet gloves, was itself an essay in theatrical presentation. He decorated his room at 47 Bridge Street with arum lilies and white lilac and became known for his devotion to the Italian Renaissance and Diaghilev's Ballets Russes.

Already aware of the importance of publicity, his parties were fully described in the local press. After one such occasion a newspaper reported that

Mr. Cecil Beaton, son of Mr. & Mrs. E. W. H. Beaton of 3 Hyde Park Street, London, W., who is an undergraduate of St. John's College, gave a (very) large party for a number of his artistic friends on Thursday. Mr. Beaton is a well-known member of Cambridge A.D.C., both as an actor and designer.

The 'artistic friends' included Steven Runciman, George Rylands, the painter Edward Le Bas and his two pretty sisters, and John Sutro, son of the play-wright, with whom Beaton collaborated on some of his early literary efforts.

His Cambridge theatrical career started in 1922, in an adaptation of Thackeray's *The Rose and the Ring*, playing Princess Angelica, which, according to *The Daily Telegraph*, he 'did very well indeed'. *The Cambridge Review* however took him and a fellow actor to task for making 'their parts unmistakably farcical!' But the concensus of the university press welcomed this talented newcomer for his 'cruel satire on the modern Society girl'.

The Marlowe Society's production of Ben Jonson's *Volpone*, the following year, was a more useful opportunity for him as designer. *The Daily Telegraph* thought his efforts were 'worthy of a London stage', and the realistic settings, in simplified Art Deco forms, won the praise of *The Observer*. Beaton had devised a system of viridian green curtains permitting scene changes with the maximum speed. The stage was divided into three areas, with an arch and an apse-like inner-stage. He used startling colour combinations, scoring special success with the Senate Room, hung in blue stencilled with silver, as background for the crimson-robed senators. The critic of *The Spectator* went so far as to pronounce that 'There is no play to be seen in London now with so beautiful a setting, except perhaps *The Beggar's Opera*'. This delighted Beaton, who was an admirer of Claude Lovat Fraser, the designer of that famous production, although the source of Beaton's own inspiration was Bakst's settings for the ballets *The Good-Humoured Ladies* and *The Sleeping Princess*.

For the A.D.C. the same year he designed a musical comedy, *The Gyp's Princess*, written by F. L. Birch and D. H. Robertson, with music by

Cecil Beaton with his mother, aunt and two sisters in London, c. 1923-4

Costume design for *The Rose and and the Ring*, 1922

D. Arundell and B. Ord. It provided Beaton with great opportunities as an artist and performer. His impersonation of Princess Tecla was described in *The Times* 'as a thing of exotic attenuation long to be remembered...the very incarnation and quintessence of all the absurdities and affectations of all the heroines that ever trod the board of a modern musical comedy'. It is clear that Beaton's affectionate knowledge of leading female performers was standing him in good stead, and the falsetto voice he adopted was said to be based on the actress Phyllis Dare. In *The Drama*, Angus MacPhail wrote of 'Mr. Beaton, whom I fairly regard as one of our greatest living actresses' having 'a serpentine grace, a feline lecherousness, which fell nothing short of perfection'. The same gift for satire was noted in the scenery and dresses, especially in his own gowns which, it was thought, 'maliciously caricatured the opulent cheapness of a musical comedy at Daly's.'

Plans to design *The Duchess of Malfi* in 1924 fell through after a row with George Rylands, but Beaton's photograph of the production in *Vogue* was itself a major event, the first of his efforts to appear in the magazine later to make him famous.

His most important theatrical event that year was the Marlowe Society's production of Luigi Pirandello's *Henry IV*, the first time it was seen in England. Beaton played the role of the Marchioness Matilda Spina, wife of the demented 'emperor', and, in the view of one critic, his was 'the outstanding performance'. *Granta*, the university magazine. however, found that his 'genius for female impersonation was not so well displayed as in previous productions', but the writer had only 'paeans of praise for the magnificent scenery and costumes'. For the juxtaposition of modern and mediaeval periods, Beaton designed the contemporary clothes starkly in black and white, a forerunner of his famous Ascot scene in *My Fair Lady*, and used costumes from an 11th century German manuscript in the British Museum for brilliant colour contrast.

It is fascinating to discover that a fellow-undergraduate, equal to Beaton in aesthetic dandyism, found 'not one blemish in this magnificent production'. Writing in the university magazine, *Cherwell*, the youthful Harold Acton was already colouring

"VOLPONE" AT CAMBRIDGE.

Acted by the Marlowe Dramatic Society.

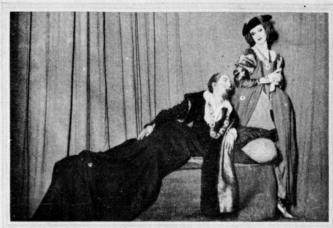

"Let's die like Romans since we have lived like Grecians"

Mosca urges Volpone to a Roman termination of his career

"How does my poor Volpone?"—The Visit of Madame

Volpone the Magnifico is visited by the loquacious Madame Would-bee

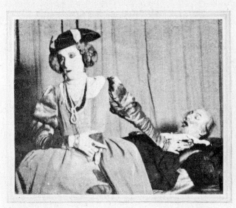

"For a desperate wit, there's Aretine"

"See here a rope of pearls"—Volpone Offering Jewels of Untold Wealth to Celia

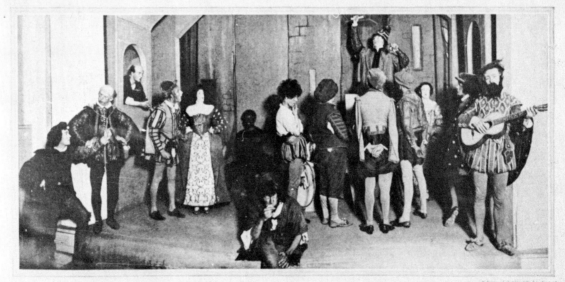

"This gives the direction; this works the effect"—Volpone's Magnificent Speech Disguised as an Apothecary, Scoto Manchuano

During last week the Marlowe Dramatic Society produced at Cambridge, in the A.D.C. Theatre, Ben Jonson's "Volpone; or, The Fox." The play was very well mounted and dressed, and acted with great spirit by the members of this society, founded in 1907 by Rupert Brooke and his friends. The above view shows in general the mode of setting out the stage. The moment depicted is where Volpone is offering his fabulous cordial to the gaping crowd

Scenes from *Volpone*, a page from *The Sphere*, 17 March 1923

Why Doesn't Charlot Send These to America?

ROLF, WITH THE BEAUTY CHORUS AS CABARET GIRLS.

IN "THE GYP'S PRINCESS": MR. J. WARRENDER AS ROLF.

MR. LE BAS AS A PEERESS.

MR. W. WILLIAMS AS A PEERESS.

MR. MINER.

MR. JEFFRESS.

MR. BLECK.

MR. BROWN.

MR. PIKE.

MR. D. WILLIAMS.

MR. CECIL BEATON AS PRINCESS TECLA.

AS VICTORY BOND, THE INGÉNUE OF THE PLAY: MR. D. D. ARUNDELL.

A BURLESQUE OF MODERN MUSICAL COMEDY: "THE GYP'S PRINCESS," AT CAMBRIDGE

The Cambridge University A.D.C.'s Christmas performance this year took the form of a burlesque entitled "The Gyp's Princess," written by F. L. Birch and D. H. Robertson. The music was by B. Ord and D. Arundell; and the scenery and dresses were designed by Mr. Cecil Beaton, who also took the leading part of Princess Tecla. Our photographs show what admirable leading ladies and members of a beauty chorus men can make when they set their minds — and theatrical costumiers — to it! We wonder if Mr. Charlot's next venture will be to take the Cambridge "ladies" over the Atlantic, and see whether Harvard or Yale can produce their like? —[*Photographs by Hills and Saunders.*]

(right) Decor design for C.B. Cochran's revue, *Streamline*, Palace Theatre, London, 1934

(left) Scenes from *The Gyp's Princess*, *The Sketch*, 9 January 1924, with Cecil Beaton as Princess Tecla (bottom left)

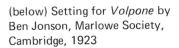

(below) Setting for *Volpone* by Ben Jonson, Marlowe Society, Cambridge, 1923

Lady Windermere's Fan by Oscar Wilde, the 1946 production at the Curran Theatre, San Francisco, designed by Cecil Beaton, in which he made his professional debut as an actor; seen here with Cornelia Otis Skinner and Estelle Winwood (Photo: Cecil Beaton)

Setting for *The Gyp's Princess*

Setting for *The Duchess of Malfi*, 1924 (unrealised)

the phrases purple. 'Mr. Beaton' he continued 'exuded a Coty-perfumed atmosphere of Roman-Venetian society'.

This first English production of Pirandello's play attracted considerable attention. The distinguished poet Humbert Wolfe reviewed it for *The Spectator* and decided that 'In Mr. Beaton, who designed the scenery and dresses, we have (unless I am much mistaken) chanced upon one who may well prove a legitimate successor to Lovat Fraser'.

The same year he celebrated his 21st birthday with a grand party at his parents' home at Hyde Park Street, London. One newspaper disclosed 'that he had designed some of the most beautiful dresses worn by guests', resulting in 'an avalanche of requests from famous society women'. 'I have been designing dresses almost from infancy', Beaton continued, 'Painting and sculpture are supposed to be my main interests, and dress designing just a little by-play, but it's becoming

something more now....'

In May 1924 he participated in the Cambridge Drawing Society, with designs for the stage and a self-portrait described as 'superbly proud'. He had been contributing regularly to *Granta* a series of caricature portraits of his stage favourites, including the American rag-time singer Ethel Levey, and Gladys Cooper.

Henry IV was undoubtedly the high mark of Beaton's Cambridge career. Later in 1924 he designed Saki's *The Watched Pot*, which, whilst described as 'brilliant and amusing', was qualified as 'inferior to his Henry IV'. With his friend, Edward Le Bas, later to win popularity as a charming neo-impressionist painter, he teamed up for an A.D.C. Smoking Concert as 'Beattie and Bass', described as 'straight from their success at the Kilburn Empire in selections from their repertoire, including Wagner and Rubinstein'.

He left Cambridge in a blaze of theatrical glory,

TERRIBLY ROUGH SKETCHES FOR THE DRESSMAKER FOR DRESSES FOR THE SAKI PLAY

CECIL BEATON, THE WATCHED POT.

IN ACT I VULPY WEARS A PERFECT DRESS OF MAGENTA. CLOSE FITTING. A CLINGING GARMENT WITH BALLOON SLEES.

AN ORANGE FEATHER FAN (VERY LUSCIOUS) "GOES WITH" HER CARROT SILK HAIR.

MRS VULPY LETTING HERSELF RIP IN HER SHEET EVENING DRESS. IT IS A MOST DARING CREATION.

CLARE ACT III CHERRY COLOUR CLOTH CLOTH & GOLD COLLAR & CUFFS. RED SHOES

IM AFRAID SHAFTESBURY AVENUE & WARDOUR STREET ARE ALREADY A MASS OF LEOPARD SKIN BUT WE MUST HAVE A LITTLE HERE. ITS SO NICE EVEN IF IT IS COMMON. CLARE ACT I BLACK CLOTH

A GIGANTIC RED BRONZE CHRYSANTHE-MUM ON HER SKINNY SHOULDER

OH SO SIMPLE.

PHILLIPA WENDELL WIG

SYBIL ACT III WITH SUNBURN COLOURED STOCKINGS.

SILKY HAIR BEAUTIFULLY BRUSHED OFF EARS. SO FRESH.

A SUMPTUOUS FLAIR.

SYBIL ACT I BLACK CLOTH WITH CRUDE EMBROIDERY LOZENGES. DULL GOLD & DULL SCARLET.

A TUBE. BEIGE CLOTH. HEAVY. TERRIBLY TIGHT & NATTY.

IN ACT III AGATHA WEARS SOMETHING A LITTLE LESS PRETTY.

A WHITE CLOTH DRESS. TUBULAR WITH FLAIR AT HEM OF SKIRT & A SCARLET COATEE. EMBROIDERED IN DULL GREEN PLUM PINK MAGENTA GOLD & COMANESQUE PATTERN.

MRS VULPY ACT III. OH SO SMART. ROUGH BLACK CLOTH TRIMMED WHITE LAWN ON CLOTH — SUNBURN STOCKING TERRIBLY SMART PATENT LEATHER SHOE.

A LITTLE THREE CORNERED HAT OF STRAW LIKE THE HATS OF THE HAGS THAT SELL FLOWERS IN PICADILLY CIRCUS TRIMMED SMARTLY WITH COCKS FEATHERS.

VULDY'S DRESS IN ACT III IS TAKEN FROM A THING IN VOGUE.

HORTENSIA ACT I DULL BLACK SILK. WITH JET TRIMMINGS IN DIAMOND SHAPE ON BOSOM & HEM OF SKIRT.

AGATHA IN ACT I SLOPPING ABOUT IN A LOT OF DAMNED FLOWERS.

IN WHITE MUSLIN WITH SASH OF SAPPHIRE + POWDER BLUE TAFFETAS.

IN ACT II HORTENSIA WEARS A VERY SEVERE CHASTE EVENING GOWN OF CLOTH OF GOLD. underneath a long fur coat.

Costume designs for Saki's
The Watched Pot, 1924

Page from *The Sketch*, 18 June
1924, showing sets and costumes
for *Henry IV*, with Cecil Beaton
as the Marchioness Matilda
Spina (bottom right)

as a member of the Footlights Revue *All The Vogue* (a prophetic title in view of his later association with the famous magazine). *The New Cambridge* declared that 'Cecil Beaton proved one of the best "leading ladies" the Footlights have had. He appears in no less than six turns and in the most ravishing creations'. In one item he impersonated Tallulah Bankhead in a skit of Noël Coward's play *Fallen Angels*. *The Daily Telegraph* wrote that Beaton had scored 'a remarkable triumph', and the *Cambridge Review* found him 'marvellous in everything he does .... he wears a series of dresses, diamanté, enormous pearls, a bustle, and a whatnot, which must be seen to be disbelieved'.

After this reception and confirmation of his theatrical gifts, including the exhibition of designs at the 1925 Wembley Exhibition, he could think only of a career connected with the stage, preferably as a designer, although ambitions to be an actor and writer lingered on. For a long time he had to be satisfied with channelling his talent in limited forms. He acted as mentor to his mother and sisters on their clothes; *The Times*, in 1925, describing a dance given by his parents, referred to Mrs. Beaton's gown of '*eau de nil* trimmed with diamanté', the ballroom decorated with pink roses, madonna lilies, rambler roses, and crimson roses in the supper room. The hand of the young Cecil Beaton surely can be detected. The family, too, reflected his interests in the list of their guests, which included such theatrical personalities as Lady Wyndham, Lady Alexander, Sir Gerald and Lady du Maurier and Mrs. Claude Lovat Fraser, widow of the brilliant young artist who had died in 1921.

The next few years were both frustrating and eventful. All Beaton's efforts to break through the

THE MOCK COURT OF HENRY IV.: LANDOLPH (G. F. A. BURGESS), HENRY IV. (D. D. ARUNDELL), THE DOCTOR AS HUGH OF CLUNY (D. E. BEVES), BERTHOLD (E. V. REYNOLDS), MATILDA AS ADELAIDE THE QUEEN MOTHER (C. W. H. BEATON), ORDOLPH (D. S. HURT), AND HAROLD (W. MILNER-BARRY.)

BESIDE THE PORTRAIT OF HER MOTHER AS MATILDA OF TUSCANY: FRIDA (W. D. A. WILLIAMS).

THE CENTRAL FIGURE IN THE PIRANDELLO PLAY: MR. D. D. ARUNDELL AS HENRY IV.

THE MARCHIONESS MATILDA SPINA—THE ORIGINAL MATILDA OF THE PAGEANT: MR. C. W. H. BEATON.

professional theatrical barrier failed, and, in a sense, this spurred on his success as a photographer. With the camera all he needed was a subject, and his family were always at hand; his first successful images were of his sisters, usually posed in the family drawing room. Soon friends of the family, or new acquaintances, sat for him, and once his work began to appear in fashionable journals there was less difficulty in finding society ladies and actresses to pose for this decorative and persuasive young man.

In his 1925 diary Beaton noted, 'I'm desperate about the necessity to work. I don't just want to take photographs, which would be a petty waste of time. But where in hell will I get the money to start an establishment where I turn out theatrical designs, paint and take photographs, all at the same time'. And on another occasion, 'I feel so annoyed, going to theatres and picture palaces and seeing others shine. I want to shine myself. I'd like to act, but what terrible parts one would get if one got a part at all'.

Beaton was determined to show his designs to C. B. Cochran, then the most successful London theatrical impresario, known for his taste and his interest in young artists. With the help of friends, an interview was arranged. The result was disastrous, and Beaton's journal records that '...he didn't look at half the things I showed him. My designs are definitely good. I feel confident about several being really original'. And later, 'I have looked through my Cochran designs and can't understand why CB didn't use any of them'.

In fact these early designs were decidedly weak, imitations of Marie Laurencin, pastiches of Lovat Fraser, colour schemes à la Bakst. Parental pressure was increasing. 'Mum came up to my room and said 'Oh dear, I do wish Cochran would accept your things. Your father is threatening to put you into Schmiegelow's'. This Danish gentleman was in the cement business and eventually Cecil, instead of going into the family concern, agreed to accept a job with Mr. Schmiegelow.

He revealed neither talent nor application for a City career. In his lunch periods he would hawk designs to publishers such as J. C. Squire at Longmans, or to theatrical producers like Nigel Playfair at the Lyric Theatre. The only offer, however, came from a Cambridge friend, Robert Herring, who asked Beaton to design the cover of his book *The President's Hat*, for the princely fee of three guineas.

The break-through came at last from *Vogue*, which in 1924 had used his *Duchess of Malfi* photograph. Beaton's posing of his sisters, disguised as Webster's Duchess, Botticelli's angels or mediaeval nuns, and friends in similar fantasies, began to attract attention.

This kept him busy at week-ends. He pointed out to his father that at Schmiegelow's he was earning one pound a week, but if he worked on photography every day he could certainly get ten pounds a week. But Mr. Beaton remained unconvinced. At the end of the summer Cecil left for a holiday in Venice, and there he contrived an

(left) Cecil Beaton in three costumes for *All the Vogue*

Drawings for *Granta*: Binnie Hale (right) and Gladys Cooper (far right)

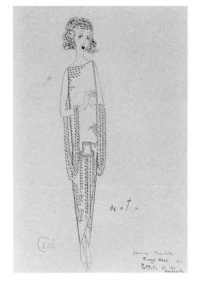 

Two early theatrical designs

introduction to Serge Diaghilev and Serge Lifar at Florian's, in the Piazza San Marco. Diaghilev examined his portfolio in silent politeness, perhaps amused to note the influence of artists he had employed for the Ballets Russes. Beaton returned from Italy determined never to go back to the City.

He was now twenty-two years old. A friend advised him to seek the friendship of the Sitwells, and, shortly afterwards, on seeing Beaton's photographs, Osbert Sitwell became his first patron. Within a year photographs of the Sitwell trio launched Beaton on an international career. Especially successful were those of Edith, posed as an 18th century beauty, a Gothic tomb carving, or a Dutch aristocrat; he found her 'the most remarkable and beautiful-looking human object I had ever seen'.

He added many glamorous creatures to his photographic net, Margot, Countess of Oxford and Asquith, Lady Ottoline Morrell, Tallulah Bankhead, and soon he was meeting everyone with any claim to social or artistic distinction.

An indication of his youthful fame is the fact that years before he designed anything for the professional theatre, the 1927 Studio publication, *Design in the Theatre*, reproduced one of his Marie Laurencin-like projects, and his earlier designs for Pirandello's *Henry IV* were shown at the 1928 Venice Biennale.

In preparation for 'professional' status, Beaton

(left) The artist's self-caricature
of a photographic session in his
mother's drawing-room

(right) One of the 'historical'
images of Edith Sitwell, 1927

Beaton's triple portrait of the
Sitwells, 1927

lost no opportunity to exercise and display his theatrical talents. Through his friend, Olga Lynn, the musician, he contributed to charity matinees. *The China Shop* (1927) consisted of a series of tableaux representing Ming, Dresden, Chelsea, Bow and Derby figures, in which Lady Diana Cooper, Viola Tree and Mrs. Dudley Ward were dressed in 'American cloth and linoleum'. Cecil Beaton himself appeared as 'Apollo'. The cast of *The Pageant of Great Lovers* (1927) included Tallulah Bankhead, Oliver Messel and his sister Mrs. Armstrong-Jones, Beverley Nichols, as well as Beaton and his sister Baba. In *Dream of Fair Women* (1928) he showed clothes of the future and, invited to write on the subject in the *Evening News* (24.2.28), he prophesied that 'Both men and women will be dressing alike...sex equality will be taken for granted.' *A Pageant of Hyde Park* (1928) is significant since Beaton and his two sisters appeared as Thomas Gainsborough and his daughters, the beginning of a fascination for the family life of the great painter, the subject of Beaton's only play.

A result of Sitwell patronage was the invitation to design *First Class Passengers Only* (1927) by Osbert and Sacheverell Sitwell. Writing from London for *Christian Science Monitor*, the well-known critic Frank Rutter noted that '. . . one of the most interesting aspects of the Sitwell play recently produced at the Arts Theatre, was the scenery designed for it by Cecil Beaton'. Another useful exercise was a parade of dresses for a revue starring Beatrice Lillie, *Charlot's Masquerade*, at the Cambridge Theatre in 1930. The same year he published *The Book of Beauty* and held his first London exhibition at Cooling Galleries, followed by a show at the Delphic Galleries, New

York, both introduced by Osbert Sitwell. By this time he was under contract to *Vogue*, which in 1928 had invited him to New York and Hollywood to photograph American personalities. One outcome of his transatlantic fame was the series of *Tableaux Vivants* staged in Chicago, with American matrons posed in imitation of such beauties in Beaton's book as Lady Lavery, Marlene

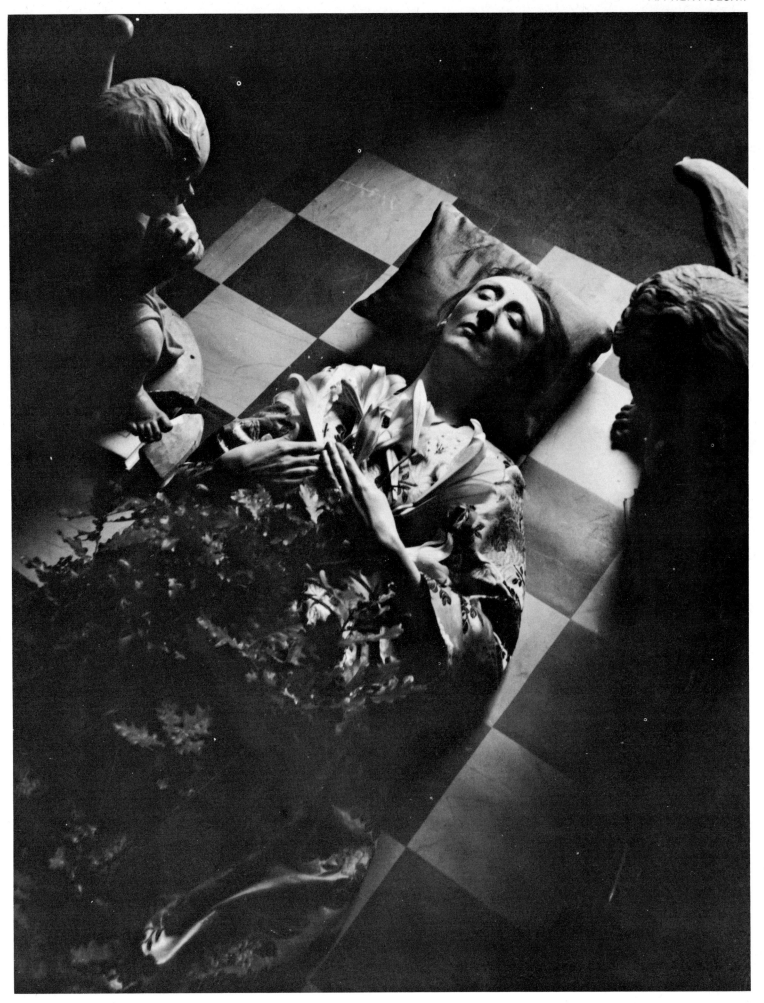

Designs for the pageant, *The China Shop*, 1927, from *Vogue*, 30 November 1927, with Cecil Beaton as Apollo (top centre)

Design for *First Class Passengers Only* by Osbert and Sacheverell Sitwell, presented at the Arts Theatre, London, 1927

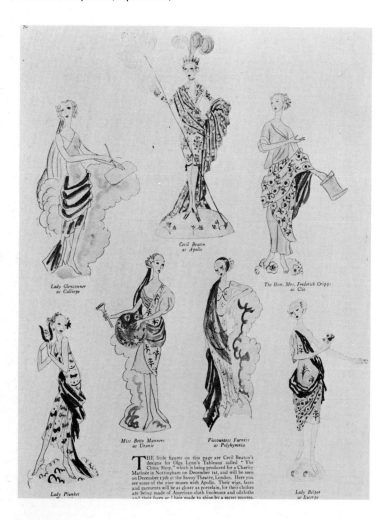

Dietrich, the Marchesa Casati, Edith Sitwell, Marion Davies and Anna May Wong.

For Beaton's 'theatrical' exercises before his professional debut, one must return to his sisters. Just as they acted as models for his early photographic compositions, so they also became live mannequins for his costumes. For a Peter Pan Ball in 1927 Baba was dressed as her 'ancestor', Lady Mary Beaton, with Nancy as lady-in-waiting to

Mary Queen of Scots. At a Catalan Party in 1929 one of them caused a sensation in a Spanish dress with an eight foot train. The same year Nancy appeared as the Empress Maria Theresa at the Countess of Carlisle's Romance of History Ball at Claridge's. The 'twenties was a great period for escapism disguised as social responsibility!

Then in 1933 came the chance for Beaton to show what he could do on a 'real' occasion, the marriage of Nancy to Sir Hugh Smiley, Bt., at the fashionable church of St. Margaret's, Westminster. It took place on 18 January, with the costumes and elaborate decorations designed to symbolize winter. To include the marriage in a study of Beaton's theatrical work is by no means incongruous. *The Tatler* reported on 25 February 1933 that 'Everyone expected something just as good as a Cochran first night. And no one was disap-

Two of Beaton's futuristic costumes from *The Sketch*, 29 February 1928: *The Bride of 1940* 'Ready for the Aeroplane Honeymoon' (right) and *Ascot gown for the year 2000* 'In Shining American Cloth' (far right)

Two pages from *Vogue*, 8 February 1928, with Beaton's ideas of clothes for the future at the *Dream of Fair Women Ball*, Claridge's Hotel, London

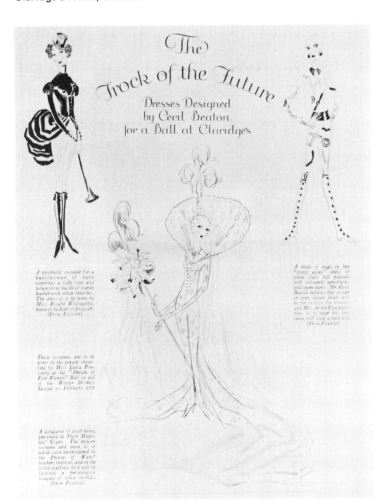 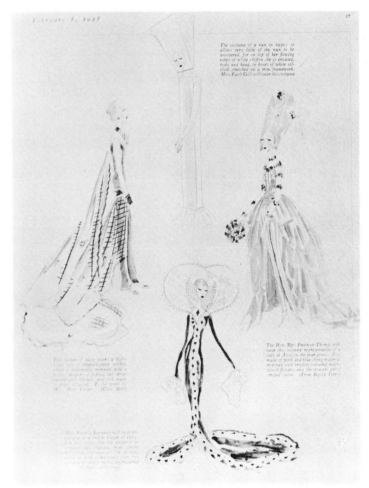

pointed....' The Marquess of Donegal, writing in a popular Sunday paper, saw 'no reason why a wedding should not be a slightly theatrical pageant'. What remains relevant is Beaton's display of his talents as a designer, creating a spectacular show in the delightful manner of a transformation scene in some fairyland', witnessed, as an American journalist stated, by 'thousands of people who lined the sidewalks of Parliament Square'.

Such observations appeared not only in the British press, but also in America, Canada, most European countries, and as far afield as Cape Town, Natal and Jamaica, accompanied by photographs showing the bride in an 'Empire gown of white chiffon, embroidered with sequins, pearls, silver, and hemmed with ermine'. Her eight bridesmaids carried white floral garlands, twelve yards

Nancy Beaton's marriage to Sir
Hugh Smiley, Bt., in 1933, the
dresses designed by Cecil Beaton
(Photograph by courtesy of
Lady Smiley)

long, the only touch of colour being the ice-blue velvet coats of the little pages. The interior of St. Margaret's continued the winter theme with 'tall silver Venetian posts, with great bouquets of chalk-white artificial flowers and palm leaves, hazel branches sprayed with chalk and frosted, flanked the main aisle of the church, and were also massed in the chancel'. At the reception the married couple 'stood under a white cage which contained a pair of pure white doves, and the house was decorated with masses of orchids, white hyacinths and lilac mingled with silver-washed bramble leaves'.

Professional debut

In most essentials Beaton's style and preferences were already set by 1934, when Cochran invited him to contribute to the revue *Streamline*. He was a mature artist, thirty years old, famous as a photographer and illustrator for international magazines, having already held exhibitions and published his first book.

Beaton's artistic style, as we have seen, was dominated by impressions of the Edwardian stage and by his memory-bank of decorative detail. From the outset of his professional work, and ever since, he has lovingly recalled and recreated his earliest stage favourites and the atmosphere of his childhood. There were also a number of subsequent influences, none more positive than the brilliant designs of Léon Bakst; Beaton's passion for the Ballets Russes dates from his schooldays. It is impossible to exaggerate the impact of his first visit to the Company and of the setting for Fokine's *Bluebird*. At school he impressed his art teacher with imitations of Bakst's daring colours, and from *The Good-Humoured Ladies* he memorized 'the undreamed-of vividness of yellow brocade, emphatic stripes and dark purple flowers, against the sombre and mysterious background of nocturnal Venice', later to guide his Cambridge setting of *Volpone*. The English artist Claude Lovat Fraser, another early influence, was himself a disciple of Bakst, as was Charles Ricketts, while two other designers who impressed the youthful Beaton, Arthur Weigall and Hugo Rumbold, were also daring colourists.

By the early 'thirties Beaton had made the acquaintance of two great Parisians, Christian Bérard and Jean Cocteau, as well as the Russian-born artist Pavel Tchelitchev, all of whom were to contribute to his mature style. Most important is Bérard, one of the theatrical geniuses of the century. In *The Glass of Fashion* (1954) Beaton describes him as 'responsible for more creative activities in the world of decor than any other person in the last twenty years'. Beaton admired the way 'he could turn a dark red plum, on an old lady's cape of moss green, both of which had hitherto been considered dowdy, into things of regal richness and grandeur'. Beaton's tribute to Tchelitchev appeared in *The Times* on 3 August 1957, following the artist's death: 'One of the most remarkable draughtsmen of the century'.

Beaton's interpretation of these influences, the broad theatrical effects of the Edwardian musical stage, the fond accumulation of childhood impressions, plus the sophisticated aesthetics of Bakst and Bérard, the surrealism of Tchelitchev, and, later, the sophisticated taste of Chanel, produced a recognisable manner of his own.

The revue *Streamline* was a typically elegant Cochran confection, with the brilliant impersonator Florence Desmond, and the Viennese dancer Tilly Losch. Early publicity listed the painters Rex Whistler, Doris Zinkeisen and Cathleen Mann as designers, adding that 'The Ladies will have a treat in some advanced fashions created by Cecil Beaton'. Cochran had either seen, or read about, Beaton's 1928 'futurist' designs. The painted flats depicted some of the artist's friends in boxes, easily recognised as Lady Diana Cooper, Lady Oxford, Olga Lynn and Lady Cunard. The last complained and had to be replaced, leading to more useful publicity. The *Daily Mail* reported that 'He [Beaton] has been so overwhelmed with applications for the part that the choosing of one will be like drawing a National Lottery'.

Two years later Cochran asked Beaton to con-

(right) Setting for *The First Shoot*, 1936

(below right) Dancers in peasant costumes for *The First Shoot*, including Sarah Churchill (far right) making her theatrical debut

Cecil Beaton as one of the ugly sisters in *Heil Cinderella*, from *The Sketch*, 14 February 1940

February 14, 1940   *The Sketch*   215

CECIL BEATON AS AN UGLY SISTER.

MR. CECIL BEATON, part-author with Mr. John Sutro of the pantomime "HEIL, CINDERELLA", devised for the entertainment of the troops and first presented at Wilton, appears as one of the Ugly Sisters and gives an amusing performance which at moments recalls the art of Douglas Byng. Our studies show him simpering, surprised, inquisitive, and self-confident, and prove that the photographer, artist, and author is also an actor of talent. "Heil, Cinderella!" has been on tour, and on Monday last, February 12, was due to begin a week's London run at the Fortune Theatre in aid of the "Comforts for the Troops" Fund.

an Edwardian photographer. The Ashton-Beaton partnership was a happy one, leading to the ballet *Apparitions*, which we shall consider in a later chapter.

It was some years before Beaton was invited to work on a complete play. Nevertheless, when he held his first exhibition of designs at the Redfern Gallery, in 1936, one critic suggested that 'Mr. Messel must look to his laurels'. This reference to the brilliant designer Oliver Messel must have struck a special chord with Beaton, who longed to reach such eminence. The *New Statesman*'s critic perceptively noted that 'He is haunted by the images of a world which he cannot remember, except perhaps from his perambulator....'

Beaton himself was determined to make a mark in the theatre. For a time the war prevented such a possibility, although in 1940, with a group of friends, he helped to write, design and perform in a pantomime, *Heil Cinderella*, which toured military bases. Later he was assigned to photographic sessions in different parts of the world, resulting in a series of books recording his experiences.

For one of his pre-war revues, Noël Coward wrote this lyric

Though Waterloo was won
Upon the playing-fields of Eton
The next war will be
Photographed and lost by Cecil Beaton.

Coward deserves at least half marks for prophecy. Beaton's war-time activities did not completely restrict theatrical work or his entry into films, as we shall see.

tribute to the revue *Follow The Sun*, this time for a light-hearted ballet called *The First Shoot*, devised by Osbert Sitwell. Another Sitwell protégé, William Walton, wrote the music, and the choreography was entrusted to Frederick Ashton. The subject could not have been more *Beatonesque*, a parody of a 1905 comedy, with a Gaiety-Girl-peeress as the central character and

DEBORAH KERR

DEBORAH KERR

Childish simplicity; an olive-green sun-ray pleated day dress, topped by a cedar-coloured tam o' shanter, worn with a fawn matinée coat

Drama and femininity combined in a tea-gown of dove-grey velvet and apricot chiffon draped crosswise to a clump of audacious scarlet geraniums

A melting Watteau-blue taffetas, very bergère—almost nursery; with meek, slender sleeves and guileless little blue dancing pumps to match

An ethereal, shimmering haze of tulle and satin and pearls in palest pastel tone accented by embroidery, and the sharp, spectrum range of the sash

EDITH EVANS

A magnificent evening gown of oyster satin and chiffon, draped with statuesque beauty. An enormous corsage of purple roses is reefed by a dangle of amethysts

EDITH EVANS

ISABEL JEANS

Cecil Beaton Photographs

(left) Beaton's photographs of the leading ladies in *Heartbreak House*, Deborah Kerr, Edith Evans and Isabel Jeans, from *Vogue*, April 1943

(right) Decor design for *Crisis in Heaven*, 1944

Costume design for Edith Evans in George Bernard Shaw's *Heartbreak House*, 1943

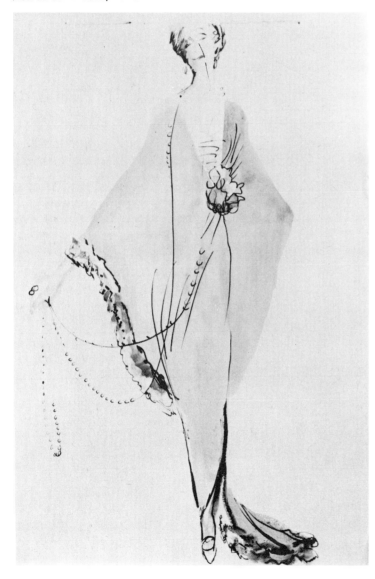

For the London stage he worked on another revue, the successful *Black Vanities* (1941), presented by George Black and starring Frances Day and Flanagan and Allen, with music by Eric Maschwitz and Cole Porter. Beaton, sharing design honours with Doris Zinkeisen and Norman

Hartnell, characteristically contributed a scene at Brighton on August Bank Holiday 1912. His dress for Miss Day won the admiration of *The Tatler*, 'white bouffant with glimpses of green and the final coup, masses of lilies of the valley all over the behind. Freudian but effective....'

Two years later he had the opportunity of designing costumes for a revival of Shaw's *Heartbreak House*, set in 1917, with a star cast including Edith Evans, Isabel Jeans, Robert Donat and Deborah Kerr. The *Evening Standard* found his contribution 'a thing of sensuous delight', but his stage activity was still regarded as something of a sideline: 'A fashionable photographer turned dress designer gives an added piquancy to the costumes'.

The following year John Gielgud chose him to design Eric Linklater's *Crisis in Heaven*, an allegorical fantasy set in the Elysian Fields and a parable of war and peace, with a wide range of historical characters. Despite Gielgud's production the play failed, although Beaton emerged with honour, treating the series of charades with gaiety and wit. *Punch* decided that the audience 'will certainly remember Mr. Cecil Beaton's sets', and A. E. Wilson, in *The Star*, who disapproved of the general goings-on, felt that 'there can be no denying the beauty of Cecil Beaton's settings'.

The designer was soon called back to narrower historical restrictions, and after a 1945 touring production of Pinero's *Dandy Dick* set in the style of the Gothic revival, he was asked to work on his first theatrical success. The production of Oscar Wilde's *Lady Windermere's Fan*, in 1945, directed by John Gielgud, was part of a lavish programme of revivals by the London firm of H. M. Tennent, calculated to lighten the gloom of post-

Decor design for *Lady Windermere's Fan*, 1945

war deprivation. Beaton noted in his journal that 'Audiences were starved for bright colours, rich silks, artificial flowers...and I too indulged my pent-up emotions in an orgy of Edwardian luxury'. As often happened with Beaton, this opportunity came about by a mixture of luck and what New Yorkers call 'chutspah'. Dining one night with John Gielgud and Binkie Beaumont of H. M. Tennent's, Beaton mourned the death of Rex Whistler the previous year. As the three discussed that designer's setting of Oscar Wilde's *An Ideal Husband*, the idea emerged to re-stage *Lady*

Windermere's Fan. To Beaumont's exclamation 'Who could direct?', Gielgud replied he was prepared to do so, and when the same question was asked about a designer, Beaton added his willingness.

Beaton says, 'This was the great and glorious moment for which I had been waiting all my life'. Walking down the Haymarket later that night with Gielgud he bubbled over with enthusiasm for rich materials, enormous upholstered furniture, Victorian decoration, glass chandeliers, parma violets and maidenhair fern. In the event, he created a

(left) A scene from the 1966 production of *Lady Windermere's
Fan*, Phoenix Theatre, London,
with Coral Browne as Mrs.
Erlynne (Photo: Cecil Beaton)

(below left) A scene from the
musical play *Saratoga*, Winter
Garden Theatre, New York, 1959
(Photo: Cecil Beaton)

Sketch for *Lady Windermere's
Fan*

Design for a staircase in *Lady
Windermere's Fan*, based on the
interior of Buckingham Palace

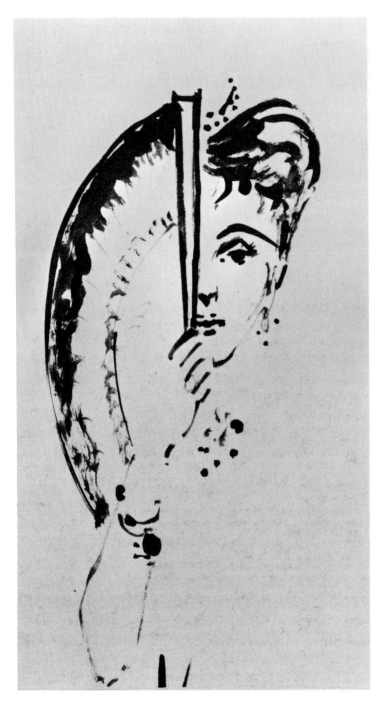

gilded drawing room with crimson velvet walls,
elaborate mouldings and stucco sculptures. The
costumes were superbly displayed by the regal
Isabel Jeans and the winsome Dorothy Hyson.
Indeed so overpowering was the visual effect that
one critic remarked, 'Oscar Wilde's epigrams
hadn't much of a chance against Cecil Beaton's
scenery'. That theatrical mandarin, James Agate,
mockingly praised the revival, giving 'precedence
to the trimmings out of compliment to Mr. Cecil
Beaton who ravishes the eye while making hay of
the realities'.

The play was well received in America the following year, when Cornelia Otis Skinner and
Estelle Winwood played the leading ladies. Brooks

Dorothy Dickson, Cathleen Nesbitt and Nuna Davey in *Our Betters* by W. Somerset Maugham, 1946

Costume design for *Our Betters*

Atkinson of the *New York Times*, wrote of 'the most luxurious settings and costumes that have been seen since the time of Louis the Fourteenth.'

Before coming to New York, the play opened at the Curran Theatre, San Francisco, where Beaton made his professional acting debut in the role of Cecil Graham, the fulfilment of an ambition long cherished but never since repeated. It appears that the American producer asked him to play the part because of difficulty in finding English actors. Beaton consulted close friends in England, and their telegram, 'Strongly advise against', decided him to accept. (Kenneth Tynan once suggested that Beaton's stage activities were 'alibis' for the fact that he always wanted to be an actor.)

Hedda Hopper, the Hollywood gossip-writer, asserted that 'it was Beaton in a Lord Dudley sort of role who made the hit. He caught the very essence of the life of that time. Funny that he never got the courage to act professionally until 6,000 miles from home'. Another critic decided that 'the whole show belongs to the ambidextrous Mr. Beaton', while to sum up his success as the designer, William Hawkes declared in the *New York World Telegram* that 'The habit of first night audiences of applauding every new scene.... was never more justified'.

If Beaton rather 'over-did' it, he can be excused by enthusiasm for the period and because this was his first real opportunity. He was, perhaps, too anxious to impress. Twenty years later, given another chance with Wilde's melodrama, he showed the steadying effect of experience, heeding James Agate's objection to an Edwardian setting, and this time shifting it back to the 1890s.

As a late-comer to the theatre and conscious of his lack of training, Beaton was keenly aware of

John Gielgud and Sybil Thorndike
in a scene from *The Return of
the Prodigal,* 1948 (Photo: Cecil
Beaton)

the status of his two major contemporaries, Oliver Messel and Rex Whistler, who were also members of his social circle. Messel's mastery over gay, decorative, rococo pastiche and Whistler's elegant architectural realism represented skilled, professional command. While it would by unjust to say that their styles influenced him, since Beaton's amalgam of personal nostalgia and desire to entertain is entirely his own, there is no denying that their success and eminence spurred him on. For years he suffered from a sense of inferiority, feeling that commissions only came his way when either or both of them had already turned them down. Beaton eventually became appreciated for his own gifts, and when Rex Whistler was tragically killed in the war, and Oliver Messel retired because of ill-health, he remained the sole representative of a particular school of English stage design.

Describing Beaton as self-taught should not imply any lack of application. Each project is preceded by detailed research, and his notebooks are crammed with sketches of every kind of decorative detail, from pieces of furniture, notes of sleeves or embroidery, hairstyles and hats, as well as colour harmonies. He allows the general plan to 'boil about' in his mind before embarking on a period of intensive work, at which point the notebooks become vital references.

During the San Francisco try-out of *Lady Windermere's Fan* Alexander Korda engaged him as an art adviser on films (see chapter 7), a position which kept him busy for the next few years. It was not until 1949 that Beaton had another major commission in the theatre. Earlier there had been some minor projects, such as Ivor Novello's revival, in 1946, of *Our Betters* by Somerset Maugham. What *Vogue* termed an 'unusual blend

(left and right) Decor designs for Sheridan's *The School for Scandal*, produced at the Old Vic, London, 1947 and at the Comédie Française, Paris, 1962

A scene from the French production of *The School for Scandal* (Photo: Cecil Beaton)

(below right) Costume design for Lady Teazle in *The School for Scandal*

of authenticity and theatrical skill' might today have been found entrancing. The anonymous lady reporter wished she could 'have grown up in the 1920s', an era she admired for its 'crudity, cynicism and perversions....'

Beaton returned to more familiar ground for the 1947 version of *Charley's Aunt*, played in London and the provinces for years after. Yet another revival came in 1948, although this time

of a rarer theatrical bird, *The Return of the Prodigal* by St. John Hankin, with the star cast of John Gielgud, Sybil Thorndike, Irene Brown and Rachel Kempson. Although Beaton was again praised for his exquisite costumes, everyone seems to have found the play a bore.

Beaton then passed through one of his periodic revulsions against the domination of memory and doubt as to the authenticity of his gifts. He felt

Eileen Herlie and Leslie Banks in
The Second Mrs. Tanqueray,
1950 (Photo: Cecil Beaton)

Cecil Beaton's portrait drawing
of Noël Coward

Joyce Carey and Lynn Fontanne
in a scene from *Quadrille*
(Photo: Cecil Beaton)

From Beaton's sketchbook on
Quadrille

that he was being used to brighten up revivals of old plays and regretted an inability to turn down work. Perhaps it would be best to break away entirely from his own life-time or the periods in which he hoped he had lived. The chance came from Laurence Olivier, then joint-director of the Old Vic Company. In 1949 he decided to present Sheridan's famous comedy *The School for Scandal*, playing opposite his wife, Vivien Leigh for the first time on the stage. The press reception for the designer was rapturous: 'inspired', 'sumptuous', 'brilliant', 'handsome and wholly appropriate'. The production was played against meticulously painted drop-cloths, with costumes inspired by Gainsborough. Osbert Lancaster, writing in *The Spectator* and denouncing the 'muddle of fantasy and realism' on the British stage, pointed to *The School for Scandal*, where

(preceding spread) Setting for
Cry of the Peacock, New York,
1950

Dress designs for *Portrait of a
Lady*, adapted from the novel
of Henry James, 1954

Jane Baxter in the revival of
Frederick Lonsdale's *Aren't We
All*, 1953 (Photo: Cecil Beaton)

'the whole scene is kept together and justified by a sense of style which never plays him [Beaton] false and which renders acceptable various flummeries, such as a super abundance of footmen and exaggerated hair-styles, which in less skilled hands might well have proved a distracting nuisance. Above all it is consistent, a virtue which can justify almost any degree of fantasy'.

Not everyone was happy; the *Manchester Guardian* found the play 'overdressed and underacted', and the Oliviers cannot have been pleased with *Vogue*'s comment that 'Mr. Beaton walks off easily with the evening's honours'. In fact, Beaton and the Oliviers ended as enemies. In his book, *The Strenuous Years 1948-1955*, Beaton declared, 'No matter how hard the Oliviers might try one day to make up for this evening's affront, I would have no further interest in them....'

He was to design Sheridan's play again for the Comédie Française, in 1962, the first British designer to work with the famous company. After the first night of the production *The Times*'s correspondent reported that 'judging from its reception it will not be the last.' The Paris reporter of *The New York Times* found it a bit extreme, the men's costumes being 'a cross between the plumes of a bird of paradise and the suit of lights of a Spanish matador'.

After the London version of *The School for Scandal*, Beaton's next major assignment was in New York, an adaptation of Jean Anouilh's *Ardèle*, renamed *Cry of the Peacock*. As so often happened with indifferent productions, Beaton stole the limelight, and the *New York Daily Mirror* found his 1912 setting 'the best thing about the play'. While in America he was invited to dress a revival of Pinero's *The Second Mrs. Tanqueray*. He re-

Costume design for *The Two Gentlemen of Verona*

searched the famous original production of 1893, which made Mrs. Patrick Campbell a star, and himself recalled the 1922 version with Gladys Cooper. Some of the critics found it all tiresome, but Beaton emerged with flying colours, although unfairly blamed for the richness of the decor. After all, Pinero's stage directions call for settings which are 'richly and tastefully decorated, elegantly and luxuriously furnished', with the women in 'sumptuous dinner gowns'.

It seemed impossible to escape the role of period decorator. Kenneth Tynan, then a youthful critic with the *Daily Sketch*, made a barbed comment on the subject: 'Modern English decor, as we have smiled at it in many a Victorian revival, really amounts to little more than a prolonged duel with icing-guns between Cecil Beaton and Oliver Messel.' It can be imagined with what joy Beaton faced the prospect of designing a new play by Noël Coward, written for their mutual friends Lynn Fontanne and Alfred Lunt. The ill-fated *Quadrille*, however, set in 1873, was dismissed as a mixture of Henry James, Oscar Wilde and Dornford Yates. It later transferred to Broadway.

Before this Beaton had the opportunity of proving his versatility in New York with a play by a new friend, Truman Capote. *The Grass Harp* (1952), a poetic drama set in the deep south, was described by one newspaper as 'the screwiest play in town'. Even Beaton was surprised at the choice of designer, but his uncharacteristic setting of a huge, wide-branched tree, filling the stage, was voted 'the most creative contribution of the year' by American drama critics.

In London, however, it was back to earlier themes, a revival of Frederick Lonsdale's comedy *Aren't We All*. The leading ladies

Decor designs for the Old Vic production of *Love's Labour's Lost*, 1954

Costume sketches for *Love's Labour's Lost*

were Jane Baxter and Marie Lohr, the latter in clothes based on Beaton's memories of his aunt. Once again the designer won the day, especially with his sunny Henley Regatta decor. 'Did they think Cecil Beaton's sumptuous settings would save it?', asked John Barber in the *Daily Express*. Beaton had set the play in 1914, an important forerunner of his designs for *My Fair Lady*.

The next year found him on Broadway again, deep in period, for an adaptation of Henry James's *Portrait of a Lady*, starring the film actress Jennifer Jones. Perhaps in reaction to typecasting, Beaton may have overdone the details; 'ostentatious' and 'florid' were some of the epithets which greeted his work.

He was to find relief in his first opportunity to design a Shakespeare play. An earlier project for *The Two Gentlemen of Verona* had collapsed, but Frith Banbury invited him to design *Love's Labour's Lost* at the Old Vic, with a cast headed by Ann Todd, John Neville and Eric Porter. All concerned were rewarded with success. Beaton sought the virtue of simplicity in the settings, with Bérardesque touches in the charming costumes.

His next play was not a revival. For Enid Bagnold's civilised drama *The Chalk Garden*, played by Gladys Cooper and Siobhan McKenna in New York in 1955, he carefully avoided exaggerated luxury. However, his predilection for absorbing and using personal details resulted in his friend Lady Diana Cooper recognising herself in the character of Mrs. St. Maugham. 'Don't think I mind', she is said to have remarked, 'but of course it's me'. The following year he worked on a vehicle for Eva Gabor, *The Little Glass Clock* by Hugh Mills. Once again it proved more of a vehicle

for the designer, and, as one critic put it, 'commendations must begin and end with Cecil Beaton's decor and costumes.'

We now reach an event in Beaton's theatrical career which can hardly be contained within the limits of a general summary. *My Fair Lady*, first seen on Broadway in 1956, was triumphantly brought to London two years later, and finally reached its apotheosis on celluloid in 1963. Since I regard all three versions as representing Beaton's finest theatrical achievement, the summation of his gifts and obsessions, I shall consider them in a separate chapter.

Angela Baddeley as Mrs. Gainsborough, with the two daughters
(Photo: Cecil Beaton)

(below right) Decor design for
The Gainsborough Girls, 1951

A literary interlude

We must now take up a curious episode in Beaton's life. As a young man he was anxious to shine as actor, writer and artist. At school and university he succeeded well enough in all three, and, in the American production of *Lady Windermere's Fan*, his professional acting debut was received with respect. The ambition to write a play remained. He had already achieved an international audience as a prolific journalist and by 1951 was the author of no less than eleven books.

The idea of a play on Gainsborough seems to

date from the 1928 pageant in which Beaton and his two sisters impersonated the painter and his daughters. Someone told him that one of the girls had gone mad, and he began to research the background. It was not his only effort at play writing; in 1948 an American newspaper reported that 'Last summer he finished a comedy which he has shown to several friends, whose enthusiastic reports indicate that it must be quite a script.' Beaton says he started writing the Gainsborough play on a train journey between Hollywood and New York, urged on by the famous theatrical couple Garson Kanin and Ruth Gordon, after he had told them the story of the Gainsborough girls. In subsequent months he turned down all offers, including the designing of the musical *Call Me Madam*. The character of Gainsborough was partly based on Beaton's father, and the closeness of his own family background made the theme of the painter's family-life attractive. Later, however, Beaton admitted that 'I had written too quickly, without knowing enough of the technique.'

In 1951 *The Gainsborough Girls*, with Laurence Hardy and Angela Baddeley as Mr. and Mrs. Gainsborough, was given a trial run at the Theatre Royal, Brighton. The plot concerned itself with the romantic adventures of the painter's daughters when the family left Bath to settle in London. The girls became rivals in love, but both ended unwed, one of them mad.

The press praised the settings and costumes, but the play itself was dismissed as 'pleasant'. Kenneth Tynan, who collaborated with Beaton on the book *Persona Grata*, in 1953, has frequently reviewed Beaton's work in the theatre and often interviewed him. In an effort to analyse Beaton's multiple ambitions, he regarded 'this strangely revealing little play' as an example of Beaton's innate simplicity, in contrast to his sophisticated image. He noted Beaton's unwillingness to settle for a single career, no matter how successful, and his apparent belief that a flair for any one of the arts promised an ability in all.

Certainly the failure of the play did not weaken his literary convictions. The production valiantly toured Newcastle, Leeds, Manchester, Swindon and Oxford, before its author decided against a London season. After 1951 he devoted himself to re-writing. Perhaps a comment in *The Stage* encouraged him: 'There is so much good material in it and it so often almost achieves its purpose, it is probable that now he has seen it in production the author will be able to strengthen his work....'

Eight years later he was ready to stage the new version, *Landscape with Figures*. The earlier production was designed in silver and grey, but now he used warmer honey tones, closer to Gainsborough's paintings. The costumes, too, were based on the artist's originals, simple dresses for the daughters, in contrast to those for the Countess of Codlington, whom Beaton depicted as a distillation of Gainsborough's grand portraits.

The new version opened in Dublin in 1959 with the actor-manager Donald Wolfit in the principal role. A diverting mixture of hamminess and egocentricity, he was a remarkable actor, but it was inevitable that two such contrasted personalities as Wolfit, with his beefy, eighteenth-century pugnacity, and Beaton, the Edwardian dandy, would clash. After the first night at the Olympia Theatre, Dublin, the critic of the *Irish*

Costume designs from Beaton's
sketchbook with (far right)
those for Gainsborough's
daughters

Design for the funeral scene in
Frederick Ashton's *Apparitions*,
Sadler's Wells Theatre, London,
1936

Costume designs for Puccini's
Turandot, Metropolitan Opera,
New York, 1961 and the Royal
Opera, London, 1963

Costume design for the Countess
of Codlington

Barbara Cavan in the role of the
Countess of Codlington
(Photo: Cecil Beaton)

Independent decided, with typical Gaelic logic, that since it was 'by no means up to Festival standard...the play could at least have started more punctually'.

The luke-warm reception prompted Wolfit to demand changes, including the re-writing of dialogue, both to suit his view of the character and, no doubt, to assist him in giving the kind of bravura performance he specialised in. When these views were made public, Beaton requested a public apology. Wolfit countered by refusing to continue the tour, for which he was contracted, and a great deal of unfortunate publicity ensued. But in the end he played the part of Gainsborough at Brighton, Wolverhampton and Newcastle, before Beaton's opus one disappeared from the stage.

One of the costumes for *Look After Lulu*, the Feydeau farce adapted by Noël Coward, New York, 1959 (Photo: Cecil Beaton)

Lulu to Coco

With the resilience which typifies the whole of his career, Beaton soon bounced back to the drawing board. In the same year as the second version of the Gainsborough play, he worked on films, his first opera and two major Broadway productions. *Look After Lulu*, however, was hardly compensation. Adapted by Noël Coward from a Feydeau farce, it proved as unwieldy as Coward's earlier *Quadrille*. Compared by *Time* to 'a brilliant tropical aquarium with the lavish flora of swirling colorful gowns and hats', Beaton's riot of Art Nouveau decoration proved less controlled than the film *Gigi*, of the previous year. Commenting on *Lulu*, Beaton says 'I thought back to Liane de Pougy and other elegant cocottes, whose gowns put out eyes at Longchamps racetrack or Maxim's', very much the world of Colette's delicious story.

The failure of the play resulted in another of those periodic revulsions against his theatrical image. 'Cecil Beaton threatens to give up Edwardian Period' ran a headline in New York, followed by the artist's advice to young designers to avoid 'the appalling period'. *Saratoga*, the same year, was his second musical after *My Fair Lady*. Adapted from an Edna Ferber novel, with music by Harold Arlen, lyrics by Johnny Mercer, and a cast led by Howard Keel, it seemed set for success. But only Beaton emerged with honour, winning the New York Critics' Award as 'Best Scenic and Costume Designer of the Year'.

For a designer it is difficult to judge productions at contract stage. With a straight play there is at least a text, and opinions can be formed about the director and cast. This is also reasonably true of opera or ballet, but far less calculable with films or musicals. *Tenderloin* must also have

seemed a winner in 1960. There were many gifted people involved, Harold Prince the producer, George Abbott and Jerome Weidman as writers, with the music of Jerry Bock (later to win fame with *Fiddler on the Roof*) and Joe Layton in charge of the dancers. The star was the distinguished actor Maurice Evans. Once again only Beaton earned unreserved praise: 'to Cecil Beaton must be given much credit for raising a singularly drab story to a semblance of excitement.'

For the next few years Beaton devoted himself to films and other aspects of the theatre. In 1962 he re-mounted *The School for Scandal* at the Comédie Française and, in 1966, designed another version of *Lady Windermere's Fan*, with a fine cast headed by Coral Browne. This production, while successful with the public, was criticised as insensitive by some reviewers. Frank Marcus, in *Plays and Players*, decided that the 'interior decorator in him has run amok', and Philip Hope-Wallace found it 'overloaded'. On the other hand, *The Times* thought it 'sumptuous', the *Evening Standard* 'dazzling', while a young lady writer in *The Sun*, under the heading 'The Importance of being Cecil Beaton', enthusiastically approved 'his pulling out some of his more madly beautiful stops.'

In the same year, 1966, Beaton had an opportunity to work with a major living writer, Ivy Compton-Burnett, or at least with the adaptor of her novel, *A Family and a Fortune*. It was an unusual challenge, since the author's strange family history, and her interpretation of it, was completely alien to Beaton's background. It resulted in one of his rare essays in abstract expressionism, decaying plum coloured walls,

Two costume sketches for *Lady Windermere's Fan*, 1966

suspended empty picture frames, stairs leading to eternity.

Beaton's last effort in the theatre was yet again a cast-iron concoction which turned out to be weak at the joints. It must have seemed to everyone a brilliant idea to base a musical on the life of the legendary Coco Chanel, impersonated by the equally legendary Katharine Hepburn and designed by their contemporary, Cecil Beaton. Pre-opening publicity took full advantage of all possibilities, Beaton was hailed as 'the most

successful stage and screen designer of the age'. He was more concerned with the enormous problem of recreating for the stage the taste and daring of one of the most remarkable fashion designers of the century. As he later pointed out, 'I knew people would criticise me for designing Chanel clothes, but if we had put authentic Chanel dresses on stage they would have looked like they came from the thrift shop'.

Not that Beaton's designs were unsuccessful; on the contrary, the opportunity to work on a

(left) Coral Browne in one of her costumes for *Lady Windermere's Fan* (Photo: Cecil Beaton)

(right) Costume designs for Katharine Hepburn as Coco

A scene from *A Family and a Fortune*, adapted from the novel by Ivy Compton-Burnett, 1966 (Photo: Cecil Beaton)

(right and below) Designs for the Little Black Dress number in *Coco*

Katharine Hepburn in the title role of *Coco* (Photo: Cecil Beaton)

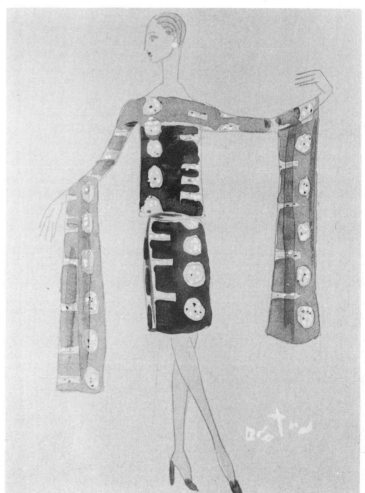

contemporary theme enabled him to exploit his sense of colour and wit. Most effective was the *Little Black Dress* number, a series of stylised variations. Inevitably many critics dismissed the million-dollar production as more of a dress parade than a musical, although Miss Hepburn won universal praise for an uncanny imperson-ation. Beaton was given the 1970 Tony Award for Costume Designing. His decor was brilliantly inventive. As in most musicals the show required rapid changes of scene, solved by a unit set on a revolving stage, so that the scene immediately moved from showroom, to the models' dressing room and to Coco's apartment. Sliding panels filled in architectural details, and a typical American engineering feat, a great circular stair-case swinging into position to meet a comple-mentary staircase sliding to meet it, was saved for the climax.

Ballet and Opera

A survey of Beaton's work in the dramatic theatre might suggest that his qualities are less suited to the lyric stage. Nostalgia for the decorative and theatrical arts of the late 19th and early 20th centuries equips him for the great naturalistic dramas of Verdi and Puccini, but could they be equally adapted to poetic impressionism? Such questions are even more important for ballet. Dance and movement demand an open, uncluttered stage. Period or psychological atmosphere cannot be established through detail, certainly nothing like the completely furnished rooms Beaton has so often dashingly recreated. In ballet the designer must be bold and positive, establishing the emotional atmosphere of the work by the evocative choice of colour and form. Beaton has always been aware of this. His earliest theatrical experiences, musical comedy, pierrot troupes, the Edwardian music-hall, all demanded an open stage. Even more important is his intimate knowledge of the Ballets Russes, from which he learned that colour and shape, in relationship to movement, are essential in ballet. From Bakst he understood that while the stage had to remain free, it was possible to frame it with painted and draped forms to create an abstract atmospheric mood, often more powerful than naturalism in its effect.

Designing for the ballet did not come naturally to Beaton, at least not in the sense that designing a period dress or room is close to his own inclinations. From Bakst and Bérard he learned the emotional and dramatic value of colour and from Tchelitchev the poetic distortion of nature. He believes that ballet offers the designer the greatest opportunities, precisely because he must achieve the maximum effect with the minimum means, requiring imagination and invention rather than the exploitation of period images or objects. The abstract nature of sound, plus the curiously irrational conventions of ballet or opera, results in an almost indefinable mixture of reality and fantasy, of naturalism and stylisation, which can communicate at the deepest level. For this reason ballet and opera offer the designer a potentially greater creative role.

In the lyric theatre, where abstract poetic fantasy is essential, the designer functions as an equal partner. It is no mere coincidence that some of the greatest modern stage designs have been for ballet. Diaghilev, who inherited the results of the late 19th century revolution of Russian stage production, raised the designer to a new prominence, equal to choreographer and musician, often into the primary role.

Beaton's work for ballet has resulted in some of his most imaginative designs, perhaps because, as with a Shakespeare play and other dramas outside his accepted range, he was forced to search for original motifs. He could not rely on the 'perambulator-eye view'. It is true that his earliest ballet, *The First Shoot*, was linked to nostalgic predilections. By good fortune his principal collaborator on that occasion, Frederick Ashton, realised that Beaton had greater potential, and this resulted in a series of ballets. Beaton and Ashton have many things in common, their life-spans, for one thing, a love and knowledge of the popular theatre earlier in the century, and the experience of the Ballets Russes. Their ballets also suggest a certain kind of romanticism, best illustrated in *Marguerite and Armand*, with its symbol of ideal, unattainable love.

In 1936 Ashton and Beaton produced their first

(left) Irina Baronova, Tatiana Riabouchinska and David Lichine in *Le Pavillon*

(right) Anton Dolin and Alicia Markova in *Camille*, 1946 (Photo: Cecil Beaton)

Margot Fonteyn and Robert Helpmann in *Apparitions*, 1936 (Photo: Cecil Beaton)

The Tenor.

(left) Costume designs for Robert Helpmann as the Tenor and for Odalisque in *Les Sirènes*

(below left) A scene from *Les Sirènes*

(right) Model for the setting of *Les Sirènes*, 1946

important joint ballet, based on a scenario by Constant Lambert, to music by Liszt. After his collaborators' recommendation, Beaton had to face the eccentric Lilian Baylis, whose gruff manner and miserliness were proverbial. Miss Baylis, more than any other single person, must be credited with the establishment of the Sadler's Wells Opera, the Royal Ballet and the National Theatre in Britain. Beaton fortunately passed muster and was informed that his fee would be £50. He was so thrilled that he would have worked for nothing.

Apparitions depicts the laudanum dreams of a romantic poet. There are four scenes, a prologue showing the poet writing in a Gothic library, followed by his visions of a ballroom, a snow-clad plain and a cavern. For the library Beaton produced an amalgam of Horace Walpole's Strawberry Hill and Beckford's Fonthill Abbey, two appropriately neo-Gothic follies of literary men. Delayed in New York, Beaton was unable to attend the dress rehearsal or the first night. Constant Lambert kept him informed:

Apparitions, you will be glad to hear, is the biggest success we have ever had at the Wells. The dress rehearsal was too depressing. Half the costumes were unfinished, the atmosphere was dead.... But when we opened there was a most marvellous atmosphere in the house, everyone was silent during the intervals, and the ballet went over as a whole with real dramatic suspense all the time.... I am sure you would have been delighted with how your work looked.

When the Sadler's Wells Ballet moved to the Royal Opera House, *Apparitions* was revived and partially redesigned in 1949. It was again repro-

duced in 1957. The larger theatre called for bolder scenic effects, an elaborated Gothic library, more colourful dresses for the dancers in the ball scene, their partners in crimson and emerald coats. At Covent Garden the snow scene was particularly effective, with its procession of purple-clad mourners.

Le Pavillon, also of 1936, was a poignant event for Beaton, since it represented his collaboration with some of Diaghilev's 'heirs', notably Boris Kochno, formerly Diaghilev's secretary, now attached to Col. de Basil's Ballets Russes de Monte Carlo. The choreographer was David Lichine, and the premiere was at the Royal Opera House, during the company's London season. The work was a trifle, with the dancers as birds, flowers, butterflies and other insects. Beaton's setting was hydrangea blue and the costumes' gauze skirts, over underskirts of varying shades of blue, were originally to be decorated with wings and flowers in brilliant colours. Kochno, however, seeing the unfinished dresses, found them so beautiful that he suggested they needed no further decoration. As a result all the audience saw was blue upon blue upon blue. 'I have since learned', Beaton comments, 'that having achieved a desired effect on paper, it is imperative to refer constantly to the original and to be extremely chary of last minute alterations.' Later he arranged for the decorations to be completed.

He was not to design another ballet for ten years, but in 1946 he worked on three. For the Metropolitan, New York, it was John Taras's *Camille* with Alicia Markova and Anton Dolin. The subject presents forward and backward currents, back to the memorable performance of his friend Greta Garbo in Cukor's famous film,

Costume design for *Les Illuminations*

Costume designs for *Les Patineurs*

Costume designs for the ballet, *Devoirs de Vacances*, 1949, for Les Ballets des Champs Elysées

and forward to Ashton's *Marguerite and Armand* in 1963, as well as the Met's production of *La Traviata* in 1966. Beaton loved the subject, but found himself puzzled over the treatment. He began to work in his usual way, immersing himself in encyclopaedic research, studying mid-19th century decoration. It was his friend Pavel Tchelitchev who taught him to distinguish between theatrical naturalism and the requirements of dance. He suggested discarding scenery and advised Beaton to invent a device to captivate the imaginations of the dancers and the audience. Tchelitchev urged him to invent a visual world which would make the audience gasp in surprise as well as recognition. 'Make everything gold and glittering, rich and dusty. All the whores should be like Victorian jewellery—make one a topaz, another amethyst, or sapphire, or ruby....' Beaton remembered this advice when he later designed

Ashton's ballet and Verdi's opera.

The ballet told the story in some detail and involved rapid changes of scenes from the ballroom to the lovers' country retreat and, finally, the bedroom. The New York press approved: 'Whatever honor the work has belongs to Cecil Beaton', pronounced John Martin in *The New York Times*, while his colleague Walter Terry in the *Herald Tribune*, found it 'as opulently beautiful as anything New York has ever seen.'

That year Beaton designed two of Ashton's ballets, *Les Sirènes* for Sadler's Wells and *Les Patineurs* for the New York Ballet Theatre. When the Sadler's Wells Ballet suggested a new joint-work, Ashton thought of Ouida's novel *Moths*, and in time this was transformed into *Les Sirènes*. Set at a sea-side resort, the ballet includes an Oriental gentleman who descends in a balloon, and, in addition to the sirens of the title, various

Two scenes from the New York
City Ballet production of
Frederick Ashton's *Les
Illuminations*, 1950

other personages emerge, including La Belle
Otero, Lady Kitty, a Spanish courtesan and a
flamboyant tenor, the last danced by Robert
Helpmann. The critics found it mildly amusing
and decided that it 'depends a great deal on the
scenery and clothes by Cecil Beaton.'

Les Patineurs, in New York, was done in a similar
spirit, the designer seeking to evoke 'the atmosphere of a Victorian, Tuppence-coloured, Hoxton-
type theatre snow-scene for Meyerbeer's sugar-
sweet music.' He produced a charming backcloth
of bare, glittering winter trees and costumes in
sharp vivid colours.

Before his next collaboration with Ashton,

Costume design for George
Balanchine's one-act version
of *Swan Lake*, 1951

Designs for one of the costumes
for Leslie Caron in the film *The
Doctor's Dilemma*, 1959

A scene from Frederick Ashton's
Casse-Noisette, Sadler's Wells
Ballet, 1951, with the 'drawn'
setting

Barbra Streisand wearing a
costume designed by Cecil
Beaton for the film *On a Clear
Day You Can See Forever*, 1970
(Photo: Cecil Beaton)

Two costume designs for *Picnic at Tintagel*, 1952

Beaton worked again with John Taras for Les Ballets des Champs Elysées, at the invitation of Boris Kochno. *Devoirs de Vacances* reflects a number of personal time-waves, the composer, William Walton, having contributed to Beaton's first ballet in 1936, while the principal dancer, Leslie Caron, was later to star in the film *Gigi*. The ballet is set in a class room suggested by Marie Rambert's rehearsals at the Mercury Theatre, London.

Christian Bérard was to have designed Ashton's *Les Illuminations*, inspired by Benjamin Britten's setting of Rimbaud's poems, but unfortunately he died in 1949, a year before the ballet was presented by the New York City Ballet. The production proved difficult. Ashton and Beaton wanted an experimental setting, everything transparent, nothing painted or solid and the costumes tawdry and disquieting. Lincoln Kirstein, art director of the company, thought in terms of clowns and even Van Gogh. Another idea followed, a supposed affinity between the German painter Paul Klee and Rimbaud, with the suggestion that the poet's birthplace, Charleville, should be presented as a child's reconstruction. Beaton even bought a building game called 'Polyforme' for the purpose. In the end they settled for a ballet within a ballet, similar to Bérard's treatment of *Les Forains* in 1945, with a troupe of pierrots impersonating Rimbaud and the real or imaginary characters in his life.

In 1951 Beaton worked on two of Tchaikovsky's ballet classics. For Balanchine's one act version of *Swan Lake* at the New York City Ballet, he designed a bleak wilderness, grey and white, inspired by 16th century German engravings, as a background for white swans and men in hunting-

73

(left) Setting for Samuel Barber's opera, *Vanessa*, first performed at the Metropolitan Opera, New York, 1958

(right) Dancers in Edwardian motoring coats for *Picnic at Tintagel*

Setting for *Soirée*, 1955

pink, while for Ashton's *Casse Noisette* at Sadler's Wells he repeated the same stylistic device of 'drawing' the backcloth. His costumes were, as always, greatly admired, but the set proved controversial. Beaton and Ashton were together again in 1952, for the New York City Ballet, in a curious work, *Picnic at Tintagel*, a version of the story of Tristram and Iseult, enacted by a group of Edwardian picnickers. From beneath their motoring coats and veils, the characters of the Celtic legend emerge, but despite its ingenuity the ballet made little mark. For the Christmas season of

1955, the Met commissioned designs for Zachary Solov's divertisement *Soirée*, with Rossini's music arranged by Benjamin Britten.

It was another eleven years before Ashton and Beaton again worked together. In the meantime Beaton had the opportunity to design the first of his three operas, once again an Edwardian theme, for Samuel Barber's *Vanessa*, with a libretto by Gian Carlo Menotti, who was also the director. Set in an unspecified country in 1905, it again called on Beaton's well-known style. First presented at the Metropolitan Opera, New York, in 1958, it was then seen at the Salzburg Festival. One American critic was impressed enough to compare the costumes to those for *My Fair Lady*, which was still running on Broadway.

His version of Puccini's last opera, *Turandot*, was also for the Met, the first production of the work in New York for 31 years. The famous conductor Leopold Stokowski was in charge of the production. Beaton had travelled widely in the Far East, returning with art treasures and notebooks full of sketches. He was concerned to find a way of suggesting the mixture of barbaric cruelty

and baroque fairy tale in the libretto, and provided a spectacular entertainment which hinted at disturbing undertones. Two incidents are remembered from the production. Stokowski insisted on honouring Puccini's request for a blood-red sunset at the rise of the first curtain, despite the designer's wish to reserve this dramatic effect for the last act. Beaton did not give way, however, in the second incident. This involved one of the ladies of the chorus unexpectedly appearing in a strange costume. Sitting in the stalls, Beaton noticed 'a large orange bottom amid an infinite number of subtle blues....'. He rushed backstage in the interval and literally ripped the offending skirt from its bodice. The lady insisted on an apology, and the appropriate trade union threatened to call out the whole chorus, but Beaton stood adamant and triumphed.

The New York critics gave his designs a cheering reception. When staged at Covent Garden, in 1963, it was equally well received. Beaton had wished to redesign the opera for London, and he would, no doubt, have changed aspects of the decor, which, in the opinion of Philip Hope-Wallace in

A scene from the London production of *Turandot*

The Guardian, did not match the 'original fantasy and high skill' of the costumes. Andrew Porter, in the *Financial Times*, found it all 'an eyeful' which reminded him of 'a Cecil B. de Mille on a limited budget', a judgement which could be applied to many British opera productions.

Beaton's latest works for the lyric stage were both on the same theme, and one he had undertaken before. The first was Ashton's ballet *Marguerite and Armand*, starring Margot Fonteyn and Rudolf Nureyev. Having previously designed *Camille* for

Structural model, with collage photographs of Rudolf Nureyev and Margot Fonteyn, for *Marguerite and Armand*

Decor design for *Marguerite and Armand*, 1963

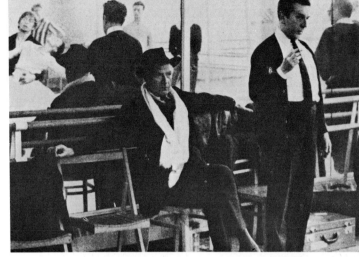

Cecil Beaton and Frederick Ashton during rehearsals for *Marguerite and Armand*, with Nureyev and Fonteyn reflected in the mirror

(below right) Costume design for Margot Fonteyn as Marguerite

another great ballerina, he was determined to find a new visual approach. Recalling the advice of Tchelitchev years previously, he searched for an idea to make the audience gasp. Working at his house in Wiltshire he stared into a flickering fire; 'My eye was caught by a Second Empire gilt fire screen. It was the period of Dumas, and it gave me the clue....' The gilded bars suggested a cage in which the unfortunate Marguerite was trapped and they also provided the stylistic theme for other properties and for the costumes. The result was a strange sculptural structure which dominated the stage.

Even more daring was the combination of photography, for the first time, with his stage work. To indicate the obsessive nature of Marguerite's love for Armand, images of Nureyev were projected onto backcloths, some distorted to reflect her dying hallucinations. There was considerable discussion about this innovation, some critics objecting to the modernness of the photographs in contrast to the Art Nouveau look of the setting. When shown in New York, an enterprising reviewer timed Marguerite's changes of costume to one every 6 minutes 40 seconds.

A new production of Verdi's opera *La Traviata*, was chosen for the opening season of the new Metropolitan Opera House in New York, in 1966. Discussions on the project had taken place between Beaton and the producer, his old friend Alfred Lunt, since 1964, and these extended until the new building was ready. Beaton hated the interior, which he amusingly describes as 'like sitting inside red dentures'. Red, however, was the colour he chose as his theme for Violetta and her friends. While everyone agreed it was sumptuous, and that he had caught the flavour of decadence in mid-

19th century Parisian social life, there were some who felt that this earlier period did not suit him.

Opera, it must be conceded, has not inspired Beaton to the elegance and originality of many of his ballets, or of the best of his work for stage and films.

Costume designs for *La Traviata*,
Metropolitan Opera, New York,
1966

Films

It may surprise admirers of *Gigi* and *My Fair Lady* to learn that Beaton has been designing for films since 1941. Even before this he attempted to make a private film with a group of friends, including John Betjeman. At the age of 24 he paid his first visit to Hollywood, commissioned by American *Vogue* to photograph the reigning goddesses, Carole Lombard, Norma Shearer, Marion Davies, Joan Crawford and Janet Gaynor. On that visit Greta Garbo resisted his photographic charms, but later they were to become close friends. In his diary for 1928, Beaton records that 'My first impressions of a film studio were so strange and fantastic that I felt I would never drain their photographic possibilities.'

Early British film commissions included costumes for Wendy Hiller in Gabriel Pascal's 1941 version of *Major Barbara*, and H. G. Wells's *Kipps*, directed by Carol Reed. In terms of period he was on familiar ground, and indeed *Vogue* asked 'Will Beaton's nostalgic creations herald an Edwardian revival?' The Art Nouveau setting for *Kipps* and the charming clothes worn by Diana Wynyard and Phyllis Calvert represent one of Beaton's many rehearsals for *My Fair Lady*. They did not please everyone, however, and the astringent James Agate, writing in *The Tatler*, pointed out that 'shop girls out for an evening walk at Folkestone in 1905 did not look as though they were going to be photographed by Cecil Beaton.'

In *Dangerous Moonlight*, famous for The Warsaw Concerto, he had a rare chance to work on contemporary clothes for the actress Sally Gray, but with *The Young Mr. Pitt*, starring Robert Donat and Robert Morley, it was back to history, an exercise in 18th century grandeur, later watered down for his Gainsborough play. *On Approval*, a delicious version of Frederick Lonsdale's comedy, is now a collector's piece for the performance by Beatrice Lillie, and in 1946 Beaton designed costumes for Lilli Palmer in *Beware of Pity*.

His real film career was initiated by the ebullient Alexander Korda, the Hungarian-born pioneer of the British film industry. Impressed by the London production of *Lady Windermere's Fan* in 1945, Korda decided that what post-war audiences wanted was opulent escapism. Beaton, however, was not happy with his experience in films. Interviewed by Ernest Betts in the *Sunday Express* at this time, he explained, 'Recently I was asked to advise on a period film. I had views on the style of the hair-dressing of the star. I drew a diagram; she came up to London three times for my instructions to be carried out. Well the weeks passed and by the time she was called for shooting, nature had stepped in and her hair was long again. I could go on for hours with stories like that.'

In New York Korda summoned Beaton to his suite in the St. Regis Hotel. 'I want to buy you' he announced. 'I don't want to be bought', Beaton retorted, 'and in any case I'm expensive'. He went on to describe his uneasiness with the medium, and that having appeared in the San Francisco production of *Lady Windermere's Fan*, he was now due to make his New York debut. Korda turned on his Hungarian charm, and, addressing the designer as 'Saisel', he pointed to fulfilled ambitions as photographer, designer, writer, actor. Surely he wanted to prove himself in films as well! Korda's trump card was a planned production of *An Ideal Husband*. Beaton extricated himself from his acting commitment and signed a contract.

Costume design for Merle Oberon in the projected film, *Manon Lescaut*

Costume design for Beatrice Lillie in *On Approval*, 1944

Agnes Lauchlan as Queen Charlotte in *The Young Mr. Pitt,* 1943

Diana Wynyard in a scene from *Kipps*, 1941 (Photo: Cecil Beaton)

Cecil Beaton with Paulette Goddard during the making of *An Ideal Husband*

(below) A scene from the film *An Ideal Husband*, 1948 (Photo: Cecil Beaton)

(below right) Paulette Goddard in one of her costumes for *An Ideal Husband* (Photo: Cecil Beaton)

An Ideal Husband was held up by a strike sparked off by the star, Paulette Goddard, bringing her own hairdresser from Hollywood. Korda decided to start on his next film, *Anna Karenina*, with Vivien Leigh and Ralph Richardson. Eventually the two films were shot simultaneously, a Guards parade in Hyde Park 1895 coinciding with a great ball in St. Petersburg.

Soon Beaton became fascinated by the opportunities for research and authenticity afforded by a well-staffed studio. He learned the special requirements of filming, the problems of lighting and technicolor, the difference between the un-edited, self-selective overall view available to theatre audiences, and the fact that the director

Vivien Leigh in the railway
station scene in *Anna Karenina*
(Photo: Cecil Beaton)

Two costume designs for Korda's
film *Anna Karenina*, 1948

and camera in films choose the details to be presented. Thus the designer finds that some special feature, of which he might be particularly proud, simply never reaches the audience. He can never be sure what the camera might pick up or what the director might select, which means that historical authenticity and perfect finish are vital.

It took some time to learn all the lessons. Reviewing *An Ideal Husband*, the critic of *The Times* found the dresses handsome, but somehow implausible; 'the designer has not given enough thought to the difference between the footlights and...the frightening intimacy of Technicolor'. Neither film succeeded. In *Anna Karenina* the

script was inadequate and the casting uneven, and, while *An Ideal Husband* was praised for Vincent Korda's sets and Beaton's costumes, once again the casting was erratic. Amid critical disapproval the *Manchester Guardian* asked, 'surely there are other ways of giving Mr. Cecil Beaton just as good opportunities?'

There was to be a gap of ten years before the next Beaton film assignment, costumes for *The Truth About Women*, in which Laurence Harvey was teamed with four leading ladies, Julie Harris, Diane Cilento, Mai Zetterling and Eva Gabor. Then came his real chance in films. He had already won international acclaim for the costumes of the

Designs for the Bois in *Gigi*, 1958

Costume design for Leslie Caron
in *Gigi*

Costume design for *Gigi*

Two costume designs for *Gigi*

Maurice Chevalier in a scene from
Gigi (Photo: Cecil Beaton)

Setting for the interior of Mrs. Higgins's house in the film version of *My Fair Lady*, 1963 (Photo: Cecil Beaton)

(left and below) Three hats worn in the film *Gigi* (Photos: Cecil Beaton)

stage version of *My Fair Lady*. The authors of that piece, Alan Jay Lerner and Fritz Loewe, decided to adapt Colette's story *Gigi* as a film musical. Beaton had met and photographed the famous writer, and he now re-read her stories to absorb their special atmosphere, to find a way of presenting the familiar period in a new manner. Research took in such famous French magazines as *Les Modes*, *Fémina*, *Le Théâtre* and *Cahiers d'Art*, resulting in notebooks full of sketches of little girls in tartan dresses, carriages in the Bois, bejewelled demi-mondaines at Maxim's.

The director, Vincente Minelli, himself an experienced designer, made known his requirements: 150 people in period costume in the Bois, with men on horseback, children playing, prams, dogs; for Maxim's, 20 dresses, resembling the Sem cartoons; at Trouville, bathing machines, period costumes, games of diabolo. Beaton worked solidly in his country house for two months before sending detailed sketches to Madame Karinska's Paris workshop. He later moved to Hollywood for studio work. Again the professionalism of the art staff was impressive.

Extras wearing ball gowns in the film *My Fair Lady* (Photo: Cecil Beaton)

Leslie Caron in *Gigi* (Photo: Cecil Beaton)

Four costume designs for *On a Clear Day You Can See Forever*, 1970

Costume design for Leslie Caron in *The Doctor's Dilemma*, 1959

(below right) Barbra Streisand in *On a Clear Day You Can See Forever* (Photo: Cecil Beaton)

He found warehouses full of furniture of every period, authentic or perfectly reproduced, with every kind of prop. Wardrobes bulged with costumes made for great films of the past. The atmosphere was calm and efficient, no one stirring a hair when requested to reproduce half a stuffed peacock for a demi-mondaine's hat, or hairstyles worn by Georges Sand and Cléo de Merode.

The result is well known. Beaton's first Hollywood film was charming, and a deserved success, earning him the 1959 Oscar for Best Costume Design.

The triumph of *Gigi*, however, was later to be eclipsed by the film version of *My Fair Lady* in 1964, as we shall see. Beaton's next film, *The Doctor's Dilemma*, was again with Leslie Caron, Dirk Bogarde playing the painter Louis Dubedat. In designing Miss Caron's costumes, he favoured the period of the Aesthetic Movement, with sumptuous Japanese kimonos based on clothes Liberty's sold at the time to arty Chelsea ladies. In one dramatic black costume she looked like the man in the Sandeman's port advertisement, complete with cape and sombrero.

His latest film, in 1970, was something of an anti-climax. The team was familiar, Vincente Minelli directing an Alan Jay Lerner musical, and *On a Clear Day You Can See Forever* had the additional benefits of Barbra Streisand and Yves Montand. The complicated story included a sequence in which the heroine finds herself removed in time to Regency Brighton, and this part of the film, which was actually shot in the fantastic Royal Pavilion, afforded Beaton the background for a series of exotic costumes. Nothing, however, could save the film from submerging with a heavy splash.

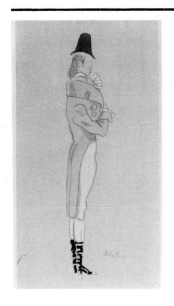   

My Fair Lady

Writing in the *Financial Times* on 18 October 1973, Alan Pryce-Jones referred to *My Fair Lady* as having 'stabilised' Beaton's name. It would be erroneous, of course, to suggest that he had to wait until the New York production of 1956, or the film released in 1963, to achieve international recognition. This had happened as long ago as 1928, after his first contract with *Vogue*, since when Beaton has hardly been out of the public eye. But in a deeper sense Pryce-Jones is right. In retrospect *My Fair Lady* must be judged as the summation of his gifts, as well as of his personal nostalgia, his memories, his earliest ambitions.

To choose him in 1956 required no special gift for spotting talent. In twenty years of professional designing he had proved his mastery of the period, and on Broadway, perhaps more than in Shaftesbury Avenue, Beaton was admired as a great showman. In 1954 and 1955 Broadway had seen *Portrait of a Lady* and *The Chalk Garden*. Eric Bentley's book on the era, *Dramatic Event*, describes the two main trends in New York as 'Kazanian realistic and the Beatonian Gorgeous'. Indeed, the year *My Fair Lady* opened was, in the phrase of *Women's Wear Daily*, the 'Beaton Season in New York'. *The Chalk Garden* was still playing, *Swan Lake* and *Illuminations* were in the repertoires respectively of the New York Ballet Centre and the Met, with a new ballet *Soirée* for the 1955 Christmas season at the latter. In addition, another play, *The Little Glass Clock*, was reported on its way.

Beaton was asked to design the costumes of *My Fair Lady*, the sets being entrusted to Oliver Smith. Earlier in his career he had often been content with such an arrangement, but later he completely opposed dividing artistic responsibility, and nothing vindicates this view more than the greater visual success of the film version, of which he was sole art director. Nevertheless, Smith's sets were unobtrusive and allowed the costumes to dominate. The original idea was to set the play at the turn of the century, but Beaton preferred the period just before the First World War, when, in fact, Shaw had written *Pygmalion*. Giving an affirmative answer to the question, 'Was it a sexy period?' Beaton was given his head, with five weeks to prepare. He says he worked in a mixture of 'impatience and lyrical enthusiasm in a 1912 world of floating chiffons, high waist lines, pointed shoes....' Never had that famous 'perambulator-eye view' focused more accurately. He wanted to recreate a world he had known, now long disappeared; 'a myriad of childhood impressions were paying dividends, haphazard pieces of the jig-saw puzzle of memory suddenly started sorting themselves out.'

As we have seen, there were many Beaton precursors set in the same period. What with his personal knowledge and long professional experience, this time he hardly needed research. Memory was his filing cabinet of documentation. Mrs. Higgins was sent off to Ascot in the dress his mother had once worn, and Eliza's grander costumes were based on the clothes of such theatrical personalities as Gertie Millar, Lily Elsie and Gaby Deslys. New York stores were raided for materials and ornaments, and when these ran out Bloomingdales produced candlewick bedspreads to be transformed into opera cloaks. Beaton's taste and inspiration proved unfailing, and every dress parade went without a single hitch. The only major costume change was Eliza's climactic gown for the ball-room scene, stripped of decoration to classic

(page 94) Julie Andrews as
Eliza in the stage production of
My Fair Lady, 1956 (Photo:
Cecil Beaton)

(right and far right) Costume
designs for *My Fair Lady*

simplicity. In the first scene the ladies emerged from the Royal Opera House in dresses based on Poiret's fashion plates; for the ballroom the designer recalled Edwardian musical comedies; whilst the sensational black and white Ascot scene was inspired by the 1910 mourning for Edward VII.

On Broadway *My Fair Lady* won six awards, including one for Beaton's costumes. The press could hardly find adequate words of praise and fashion designers exploited a new trend. Along Madison and Park Avenues Beaton was haunted by ghosts of relatives or beloved Edwardian actresses in the shop windows.

In preparation for the London production in 1958, he added twenty new costumes and broader decorative effects. 'When I first designed the costumes they were avant-garde, so to speak, now fashion had caught up with me.' The critic of *The Times* noted these changes but decided that, 'though broadened out into spectacle, they express a sense of the period in which the comedy is set.' The Ascot scene was a great *coup de théâtre*, the stylisation of the fantastic black and white dresses cunningly produced to imitate one of Beaton's photographs frozen into a magnificent magpie tableau. This worked much better on the stage, with the audience occupying the same space as the human sculpture. In the cinema the witty imitation of a photographic image was somewhat vitiated by the medium. A comment in *The Sunday Times* echoed the views of the press and the public that 'The costumes he created for it have a luxury, elegance and beauty that have largely contributed to its being the most successful musical play of the century.'

It must be rare, if not unique, for the same

"MY FAIR LADY" ASCOT COSTUMES.

BEATON

designer successfully to contribute to the stage and film versions of a landmark in modern entertainment. For the film, however, Beaton was in complete control. While his mastery of costume was indisputable, previous stage settings had sometimes aroused misgivings, and he had less experience in film decor. Beaton himself once wrote, 'I believe my natural instinct is for costume rather than sets.' The veteran film director, George Cukor, was in charge, and Beaton took him on a tour of London to suggest settings. They went not merely to the Royal Opera House at Covent Garden, and the famous market, with the imposing portico of St. Paul's Church, but also further afield to Bedford Park, Norman Shaw's pioneer garden-suburb, houses by C. F. A. Voysey and the mansions of Fitzjohn's Avenue, Hampstead. Beaton hoped that the film would use authentic sites, but this was not to be, and in February 1963 he installed himself at

Warner Brothers studio in Hollywood, worried as how to achieve authenticity.

The piazza at Covent Garden was realistically recreated, with poetic license in the elongation of proportions, distant buildings made narrow and tall, the columns of the church drawn closer together. Having decided to set the film in 1910, Beaton took as his stylistic theme British Art Nouveau, the linear version favoured by the brilliant Scottish architect Charles Rennie Mackintosh, although for the interiors he drew upon the work of Voysey and Hugh Baillie-Scott. Of the twenty sets in the film, the principal background, Professor Higgins's establishment in Wimpole Street, was based on an actual house in the street, one occupied by Beaton's doctor. Mrs. Higgins's domain was pure invention, an Art Nouveau confection influenced by the late Victorian illustrators Kate Greenaway and Walter Crane. For the furniture and ornaments the problem was finding

(left and below) Costume designs
for *My Fair Lady*

Beaton's sketched portrait of
Audrey Hepburn as Eliza

The Ascot scene in the stage
version of *My Fair Lady* (Photo:
Cecil Beaton)

originals to be copied. Hollywood antique shops had few suitable examples, and Beaton toured the junk shops, occasionally finding washstands, export oriental furniture, old gramophones, period biscuit and cigar boxes, and even a large carved dog's head in the form of a letter rack. Hardware shops were ransacked for out-of-date doorknobs, handles, locks and bathroom fittings. London supplied the wallpapers with Coles using original 1910 blocks and Sandersons printing copies of William Morris designs.

In his own record of the film, Beaton describes the endless decisions facing the art director.

Because half-a-dozen people wanted me at the same time, I felt hounded. Gene appeared with a rough draft of a portrait of Gladys Cooper, done in Pre-Raphaelite style, for correction. 'Make the dove a lily. Make the hair fuller. Paint the whole thing more meticulously—less impressionistic'. He showed me some blueprints for the Embassy staircase. 'Make the tops of the panels semi-circular—not squashed.' Bob Richards arrived from the Men's Wardrobe with samples for Rex's dressing-gown and

(right) Beaton's sketches of Rex
Harrison and Stanley Holloway

Design for Eliza's Ascot costume

(preceding spread) Ascot costumes for *My Fair Lady* (Photo: Cecil Beaton)

(below) Ascot costumes for *My Fair Lady* (Photo: Cecil Beaton)

(right) The film version of the Ascot scene in *My Fair Lady* (Photo: Cecil Beaton)

pyjamas. He said 'Do you think, as Rex sweats so much, two pyjamas are enough?' Joe about artificial flowers from Paris being mistaken by Customs for real and consequently being impounded: Jim about more doorknobs. and Robbie about a prop handkerchief for wiping Audrey's nose. A decision: 'No' to the swans on Eliza's bedpost, but 'Yes' to having the cretonne curtains of the same design as the wallpaper behind the bedhead. George Hopkins told me he has bought this silver bed from a woman who had asked $20,000 for the pair, but accepted $700 for one. Audrey, herself, was waiting for me to direct the various hairstyles she would wear in the interim stages between being the Cockney flower seller and the resplendent butterfly. Tough going . . . .

One fascinating consideration arises from the transition from stage to screen. Stage naturalism not only requires stylisation, it must accept that the audience cannot be fooled. They know they are in a place of entertainment, that what they see,

framed by the proscenium arch, is not reality. Neither is a film, but it makes a greater effort to appear real, in some cases showing real streets and buildings, even rooms that exist somewhere. Audiences cannot always distinguish between reality and studio re-creation. While the stage always represents make-believe, the cinema produces a counterpoint of fantasy and reality. Thus, in the stage version of *My Fair Lady*, the stylisation of the Ascot costumes and the frozen grouping may have been at variance with the period realism of other dresses, but this would not have disturbed the audience. In a film, such stylistic clashes are dangerous. After all, great care had been taken, especially in Higgins's sound laboratory and the rest of his establishment, to create a believable, lived-in house. Beaton was well aware of the problem, and the contrast of the painted sets in Olivier's film of *Henry V* with the battle scenes

Audrey Hepburn in Eliza's Ascot dress, *My Fair Lady* (Photo: Cecil Beaton)

Audrey Hepburn in the ball-dress for the film of *My Fair Lady* (Photo: Cecil Beaton)

Audrey Hepburn dressed for the ball (far left) and in another costume (left) from *My Fair Lady* (Photos: Cecil Beaton); and Beaton's portrait (below) of her as the Cockney flower-seller

Beaton's impression of the ballroom sequence in the film of *My Fair Lady*

in the real outdoors, which they followed, was a constant reminder. In the end he got away with it, and while the Ascot scene came as a surprise, even a shock, to the audience, this was as planned.

'I am pessimistic by nature and always antici-

pate disaster', Beaton says. Never were such intimations of failure less justified. Rather, it can be said, the film of *My Fair Lady* ensures Beaton's immortality as a stage designer. If the reception of the stage versions was rapturous, it was as nothing

Costume designs for *My Fair Lady*

to the acclaim of the critics and public which greeted the film.

Beaton emerged as one of the 'stars' of the film, rewarded with two Oscars, one for costume design, the other for art direction. Some critics thought the designs remained 'stagey', but *Newsweek* judged the total visual quality of the film as 'a work of genius' and Isabel Quigly in *The Spectator* considered that the designs amounted to 'historical comment'.

In their totality, Beaton's various contributions to the stage and film versions of *My Fair Lady* represent his masterpiece. He once remarked, 'There is no formula for success .... the element of the unknown is always present to make or mar your effects .... but when all the elements fuse and an entity is created, then all the heartburns seem to have been worth while.' It is, perhaps, only with *My Fair Lady* that he fully achieved this artistic entity. It completely represents his notion of the theatre, 'which at its finest should be an opulent cornucopia showering the spectator with golden illusions not to be found at home.'

Within this aim Beaton has been one of the great entertainers of the century.

Productions designed by Cecil Beaton

(Unless otherwise stated, the artist was responsible for both decor and costumes. Release dates are given for films).

1922 *The Rose and the Ring*
by H. M. Thackeray, dramatised by E. Sidgwick
ADC Theatre, Cambridge
costumes

1923 *Volpone*
by Ben Jonson
Marlowe Dramatic Society, Cambridge
settings

The Gyp's Princess
by F. L. Birch and D. H. Robertson; music by
D. Arundell and B. Ord
ADC Theatre, Cambridge

1924 *The Watched Pot*
by Saki (H. H. Munro)
ADC Theatre, Cambridge

Henry IV
by Luigi Pirandello
Marlowe Dramatic Society, Cambridge

ADC Smoking Concert
Cambridge
costumes

1925 *All the Vogue*—Footlights Revue
New Theatre, Cambridge
costumes

1927 *The China Shop*
charity matinee arranged by Olga Lynn
Savoy Theatre, London
costumes

First Class Passengers Only
by Osbert and Sacheverell Sitwell
Arts Theatre, London

A Pageant of Great Lovers
charity matinee arranged by Olga Lynn
New Theatre, London
costumes

1928 *A Pageant of Hyde Park* 1765–1928
charity matinee arranged by Olga Lynn
Dalys Theatre, London
costumes

1930 *Charlot's Masquerade*
revue with Beatrice Lillie
Cambridge Theatre, London
costumes for mannequin parade

1934 *Streamline*—C. B. Cochran revue
with Florence Desmond and Tilly Losch
Palace Theatre, London
costumes (other designers Doris Zinkeisen,
Rex Whistler, Cathleen Mann)

1936 *Follow the Sun*—C. B. Cochran revue
Adelphi Theatre, London
decor and costumes for the ballet *The First Shoot*
by Osbert Sitwell, choreography Frederick Ashton,
music William Walton

Le Pavillon
ballet by Boris Kochno and David Lichine, music
Alexander Borodin, Col. W. de Basil's Ballets
Russes de Monte Carlo
premiere Royal Opera House, London

Apparitions
ballet by Frederick Ashton, music Franz Liszt
Vic-Wells Ballet, with Margot Fonteyn and
Robert Helpmann
Sadler's Wells Theatre, London

1940 *Heil Cinderella*
by Cecil Beaton and John Sutro
pantomime for the Wilton House Company tour

1941 *Major Barbara*, film based on George Bernard
Shaw's play
directed by Gabriel Pascal
with Wendy Hiller, Deborah Kerr, Rex Harrison,
costumes

Black Vanities—George Black revue
with Frances Day, Flanagan and Allen
Victoria Palace, London
costumes (other designers Doris Zinkeisen,
Norman Hartnell)

Kipps, film based on H. G. Wells's novel
directed by Carol Reed
with Diana Wynyard, Michael Redgrave

Dangerous Moonlight, film
directed by Brian Desmond Hurst
with Sally Gray, Anton Walbrook
costumes

1942 *The Young Mr. Pitt*, film
directed by Carol Reed
with Robert Donat, Robert Morley
costumes

1943 *Heartbreak House*
by George Bernard Shaw
with Deborah Kerr, Isabel Jeans, Edith Evans,
Robert Donat
Cambridge Theatre, London
costumes

1944 *Crisis in Heaven*
by Eric Linklater
directed by John Gielgud
with Dorothy Dickson, Adele Dixon
Lyric Theatre, London

On Approval, film based on the play by Frederick
Lonsdale
directed by Clive Brook
with Beatrice Lillie, Googie Withers, Roland
Culver and Clive Brook
costumes

1945 *Dandy Dick*
by Arthur Wing Pinero
with Sidney Howard, A. E. Matthews
touring production

Lady Windermere's Fan
by Oscar Wilde
directed by John Gielgud
with Isabel Jeans, Athene Seyler, Dorothy Hyson
Haymarket Theatre, London

1946 *Lady Windermere's Fan*
by Oscar Wilde
with Cornelia Otis Skinner, Estelle Winwood,
Cecil Beaton
Curran Theatre, San Francisco (later New York)

Our Betters
by W. Somerset Maugham
directed by Ivor Novello
with Dorothy Dickson, Cathleen Nesbitt,
Max Adrian
Playhouse Theatre, London

Beware of Pity, film
directed by Maurice Elvey
with Lilli Palmer
costumes

Camille
ballet by John Taras, music Franz Schubert
with Alicia Markova and Anton Dolin
Metropolitan Opera House, New York

Les Sirènes
ballet by Frederick Ashton, music Lord Berners
Sadler's Wells Ballet, with Margot Fonteyn,
Robert Helpmann
Royal Opera House, London

Les Patineurs
ballet by Frederick Ashton, music Giacomo
Meyerbeer
Ballet Theatre, Broadway Theatre, New York

1947 *Charley's Aunt*
by Brandon Thomas
Palace Theatre, London

1948 *The Return of the Prodigal*
by St. John Hankin
with John Gielgud, Sybil Thorndike
Globe Theatre, London

An Ideal Husband, film based on the play by
Oscar Wilde
directed by Alexander Korda
with Paulette Goddard, Michael Wilding, Diana
Wynyard, Glynis Johns
costumes

Anna Karenina, film based on the novel by Leo
Tolstoy
directed by Julien Duvivier
with Vivien Leigh, Ralph Richardson
costumes

1949 *The School for Scandal*
by Richard Brinsley Sheridan
with Laurence Olivier, Vivien Leigh
Old Vic Company, New Theatre, London

Devoirs de Vacances
ballet by John Taras, music William Walton
Les Ballets des Champs Elysées, with Leslie Caron

1950 *Cry of the Peacock*
by Cecil Robson, based on *Ardèle ou La Marguerite*
by Jean Anouilh
Mansfield Theatre, New York

The Second Mrs. Tanqueray
by Arthur Wing Pinero
with Eileen Herlie, Leslie Banks
Haymarket Theatre, London

Les Illuminations
ballet by Frederick Ashton, music Benjamin
Britten
New York City Ballet, City Center, New York

1951 *Swan Lake* (one-act version)
ballet by George Balanchine, music Peter
Tchaikovsky
New York City Ballet, City Center, New York

Our Lady's Tumbler
by Ronald Duncan
Salisbury Cathedral

Casse-Noisette
ballet by Frederick Ashton, music Peter
Tchaikovsky
Sadler's Wells Theatre Ballet
Royal Opera House, London

The Gainsborough Girls
by Cecil Beaton
with Angela Baddeley, Laurence Hardy
Theatre Royal, Brighton

1952 *Quadrille*
by Noël Coward
with Alfred Lunt, Lynn Fontanne
Phoenix Theatre, London

Picnic at Tintagel
ballet by Frederick Ashton, music Arnold Bax
New York City Ballet, City Center, New York

The Grass Harp
by Truman Capote
Martin Beck Theatre, New York

1953 *Aren't We All*
by Frederick Lonsdale
with Jane Baxter, Marie Lohr
Haymarket Theatre, London

1954 *Portrait of a Lady*
by William Archibald, based on the novel by
Henry James
with Jennifer Jones, Cathleen Nesbitt, Robert
Flemyng
ANTA Theatre, New York

Love's Labour's Lost
by William Shakespeare
with Ann Todd, John Neville, Eric Porter
Old Vic Theatre, London

Quadrille
by Noël Coward
with Alfred Lunt, Lynn Fontanne, Edna Best,
Brian Aherne
Coronet Theatre, New York

1955 *The Chalk Garden*
by Enid Bagnold
with Gladys Cooper, Siobhan McKenna
Ethel Barrymore Theatre, New York

Soirée
ballet by Zachary Solov, music Gioacchino Rossini
(arranged by Benjamin Britten)
Metropolitan Opera House, New York

1956 *My Fair Lady*
by Alan Jay Lerner, based on George Bernard
Shaw's play *Pygmalion*
music Frederick Loewe
with Rex Harrison, Julie Andrews, Stanley
Holloway, Zena Dare
Mark Hellinger Theatre, New York
costumes

The Little Glass Clock
by Hugh Mills
with Eva Gabor
John Golden Theatre, New York

1958 *Gigi*, film based on a story by Colette
directed by Vincente Minelli
with Leslie Caron, Maurice Chevalier, Hermione
Gingold

My Fair Lady
by Alan Jay Lerner, based on George Bernard
Shaw's play *Pygmalion*
music Frederick Loewe
with Rex Harrison, Julie Andrews, Stanley
Holloway, Zena Dare
Drury Lane Theatre, London
costumes

The Truth About Women, film
directed by Sydney and Muriel Box
with Laurence Harvey, Julie Harris, Diane
Cilento, Mai Zetterling, Eva Gabor
costumes

Vanessa
opera by Samuel Barber, libretto Gian Carlo
Menotti
directed by Gian Carlo Menotti
with Eleanor Steber, Nicolai Gedda, Rosalind Elias,
Giorgio Tozzi, Regina Resnik
Metropolitan Opera House, New York

1959 *Landscape with Figures* (new version of *The
Gainsborough Girls*)
by Cecil Beaton
with Donald Wolfit
Olympia Theatre, Dublin

Saratoga
from the novel by Edna Ferber
with Howard Keel, Carol Lawrence
Winter Garden Theatre, New York

Look After Lulu
by Noël Coward, adapted from Georges Feydeau's
Occupe toi d'Amélie
with Tammy Grimes, Roddy McDowell
Henry Miller's Theatre, New York

The Doctor's Dilemma, film based on the play by
George Bernard Shaw
directed by Anthony Asquith
with Leslie Caron, Dirk Bogarde
costumes

1960 *The Importance of Being Earnest*
by Oscar Wilde
illustrations for the Folio Society edition

Tenderloin
by George Abbott and Jerome Weidman, based on
the novel by Samuel Hopkins Adams, music Jerry
Bock
with Maurice Evans
Forty-Sixth Street Theatre, New York

Dear Liar
by Jerome Kilty, a dramatised version of the
correspondence between Ellen Terry and George
Bernard Shaw
with Katharine Cornell and Brian Aherne
USA tour
costumes

1961 *Turandot*
opera by Giacomo Puccini
with Birgit Nilsson, Franco Corelli, Anna Moffo
Metropolitan Opera House, New York

1962 *The School for Scandal*
by Richard Brinsley Sheridan
Comédie Française, Paris

1963 *Turandot*
opera by Giacomo Puccini
with Amy Shuard, Bruno Prevedi, Raina
Kabaivanska
Royal Opera House, London

Marguerite and Armand
ballet by Frederick Ashton, music Franz Liszt
Royal Ballet Company, with Margot Fonteyn and
Rudolf Nureyev
Royal Opera House, London

My Fair Lady, film
directed by George Cukor
with Rex Harrison, Audrey Hepburn, Stanley
Holloway, Gladys Cooper

1966 *La Traviata*
opera by Giuseppe Verdi
directed by Alfred Lunt
with Anna Moffo, Bruno Prevedi, Robert Merrill
Metropolitan Opera House, New York

Lady Windermere's Fan
by Oscar Wilde

with Coral Browne, Isabel Jeans
Phoenix Theatre, London

A Family and a Fortune
by Julian Mitchell, based on the novel by Ivy
Compton-Burnett
with Catherine Lacey
Yvonne Arnaud Theatre, Guildford

1969 *Coco*
by Alan Jay Lerner, music André Previn
with Katharine Hepburn
Mark Hellinger Theatre, New York

1970 *On a Clear Day You Can See Forever*, film
directed by Vincente Minelli
with Barbra Streisand, Yves Montand
costumes

PROJECTS

Adriana Lecouvreur, opera by Francesco Cilèa
Metropolitan Opera, New York

Cyrano de Bergerac by Edmond Rostand
to be directed by José Ferrer

The Two Gentlemen of Verona by William
Shakespeare
Old Vic Company, London

Madama Butterfly, opera by Giacomo Puccini

Manon Lescaut, film with Merle Oberon

Ballet based on Elisabeth and Mary, by Martha
Graham

Exhibitions

1925 International Exhibition, Wembley—British
Drama League exhibition of stage designs

1928 Venice Biennale—designs for Pirandello's *Henry IV*

1929 Everglades Club, Palm Beach

Elsie de Wolfe Galleries, New York

1930 Cooling Galleries, London

1931 Delphic Galleries, New York

1936 Redfern Gallery, London—designs for three
ballets

1937 Carroll Carstairs Gallery, New York

1942 Estudio do Spu, Lisbon

1951 Sagittarius Gallery, New York

1957 Arts Council, Cambridge—*Modern English
Theatre Design*

1958 Redfern Gallery, London—designs for *My Fair
Lady*

1964 Redfern Gallery, London

1966 Lefevre Gallery, London—paintings

1968 Palm Beach Gallery, Miami

Wright Hepburn Gallery, London—stage designs

1969 National Portrait Gallery, London—photographic
portraits, 1928-1968

Museum of the City of New York—photographic
portraits, 1928-1968

1970 Palm Beach Gallery, Miami

1971 Victoria and Albert Museum, London—*Fashion:
An Anthology*

1972 Palm Beach Gallery, Miami

1974 Kodak House, London—photographic retrospective;
later toured

Annely Juda Gallery, London—*Theatre*, collective
exhibition of 20th century stage design (later
shown in Cologne, Basle, Milan).

Bibliography

Amberg, George	*Art in Modern Ballet*, Pantheon, New York; Routledge, London 1946
Barsacq, Léon	*Le Décor du Film*, Cinema Club, Seghers, Paris 1970
Beaton, Cecil	*The Book of Beauty*, Duckworth, London 1930
	Cecil Beaton's Scrapbook, Batsford, London 1937
	Cecil Beaton's New York, Batsford, London 1938
	Photobiography, Odhams, London 1951
	Ballet, Wingate, London 1951
	Persona Grata, with Kenneth Tynan, Wingate, London 1953
	The Glass of Fashion, Weidenfeld & Nicolson, London 1954
	Scenery and Costume Design for the Ballet, *New York Times*, 29.7.1956, reprinted in *Some Designs for Stage and Screen* 1961
	Designs for the Theatre by Rex Whistler, *The Masque*, Curtain Press, London 1957 (with James Laver and Lawrence Whistler)
	Cecil Beaton's Diaries: 1922-1929 The Wandering Years, Weidenfeld & Nicolson, London 1961
	Cecil Beaton's Fair Lady, Weidenfeld & Nicolson, London 1964
	Cecil Beaton's Diaries: 1939-1944 The Years Between, Weidenfeld & Nicolson, London 1965
	Cecil Beaton's Diaries: 1944-1948 The Happy Years, Weidenfeld & Nicolson, London 1972
	Cecil Beaton's Diaries: 1948-1955 The Strenuous Years, Weidenfeld & Nicolson, London 1973
Beaumont, Cyril W.	Design for the Ballet, *The Studio*, London 1937
	Ballet Design Past and Present, *The Studio*, London 1946
Bentley, Eric	*Dramatic Event*, Dobson, London 1957
Buckle, Richard	*Modern Ballet Design*, Adam & Charles Black, London 1965
Coratheie, Elisabethe	Cecil Beaton, *Theatre World*, June 1965
Hainaux, René	*Stage Design Throughout the World Since 1935*, Harrap, London 1947
	Stage Design Throughout the World Since 1960, Harrap, London 1973
Holme, Geoffrey	Design in the Theatre, *The Studio*, London 1927
Larson, Orville K.	*Some Designs for Stage and Screen*, Michigan State University Press, 1961
Morley, Sheridan	*Theatre 73*, Hutchinson, London 1973
Spencer, Charles	*Léon Bakst*, Academy Editions, London 1973
	The Stage-Struck Cecil Beaton, *Theatre 73*, edited by Sheridan Morley, Hutchinson, London 1973
Vogue	issues from 1924 to 1973
Whitworth, Geoffrey	Theatre in Action, *The Studio*, London and New York 1939